THE CHRISTIAN

Christian Belief
for Everyone

Book 5

THE CHRISTIAN LIFE
AND HOPE

Alister McGrath

First published in Great Britain in 2015

Society for Promoting Christian Knowledge
36 Causton Street
London SW1P 4ST
www.spck.org.uk

British Library Cataloguing-in-Publication Data
A catalogue record for this book is available from the British Library

ISBN 978–0–281–06841–8
eBook ISBN 978–0–281–06842–5

Typeset by Graphicraft Limited, Hong Kong
First printed in Great Britain by Ashford Colour Press
Subsequently digitally printed in Great Britain

eBook by Graphicraft Limited, Hong Kong

Produced on paper from sustainable forests

Contents

v

Introduction

Someone once asked me why I liked preaching so much. I hesitated before answering as I actually find preaching very challenging, if also deeply rewarding. My answer lies in some words of C. S. Lewis, who declared that the best test of whether you had understood something yourself was whether you could translate it into ordinary language. As a professional theologian I find it relatively easy to talk about the core ideas of the Christian faith using professional jargon. But preaching forces me to translate those ideas into the cultural vernacular, figure out what analogies and images will help me make my point and the difference those ideas will make to the way we live the Christian life.

But there's another point. In preaching to my congregations I'm really preaching to myself. I constantly need to challenge myself as to whether I have really understood and appreciated the core themes of the Christian faith. One of my favourite sermon stories concerns the great Baptist preacher C. H. Spurgeon. Spurgeon was regarded as one of the greatest preachers of his age, and was especially noted for his classic sermon 'Forgiveness', first preached in May 1855. Like all of Spurgeon's sermons, this was widely copied and disseminated.

The story tells of how Spurgeon went on vacation to the west of England. On Sunday morning he attended the local Baptist church and heard a powerful and challenging sermon on forgiveness that brought tears to his eyes. Afterwards he introduced himself to the preacher, who was stunned to realize that Spurgeon had been in the congregation. Shamefacedly he confessed that he had 'borrowed' – without, it seems, due acknowledgement – Spurgeon's own classic sermon on forgiveness that very morning! Spurgeon waved away the preacher's apology, declaring: 'I needed somebody to preach that sermon to me.'

That's the way I feel as well. As I prepare my sermons, I ask myself what I need to hear from the biblical passage in question and what I need to understand more about the great doctrinal themes I will be exploring in my sermon. I'm preaching to myself. Sometimes my own sermons make me feel uncomfortable. Surely that's a good thing? Yet at other times they make me feel excited – above all when I open up the great theme of hope, the subject of this book. For hope is not primarily about understanding something to be true; it's about grasping a vision of reality that reassures us there is a 'big picture' to life – not just a series of disconnected snapshots. And above all it reassures us that there is a link between this world and another, in which we have a place.

In this final volume in the Christian Belief for Everyone series we begin by picking up where the previous one left off. *The Spirit of Grace* ended with reflection on the nature of the Church; this volume opens with exploration of the sacraments. What use are they in helping us to live the Christian life? What do Christians believe about them, and what are they meant to do with them?

We then move on in Chapters 2 and 3 to look at the major theme of the final section of the creeds: the hope of resurrection. Why is this theme of resurrection so important? What is the Christian vision of heaven all about? How does it relate to everyday life and to the worship of the Church? Some

Christians feel uneasy about this idea, believing that it leads to a lack of engagement with the world around us. Yet when rightly understood it turns out to be energizing. The Christian hope – like the Christian faith itself – is not rooted in some kind of wishful thinking or groundless optimism in the goodness of human nature but in a loving and trustworthy God who refuses to let violence, death and destruction have the final word. The Christian vision of hope is not just about a future consolation for the suffering, pain and disappointments of life but about our restoration to the life God always wanted for us, and entered into our history in order that we might have.

This leads us to think more closely about the Christian life. What does it mean to live 'between the times'? How can we go further up and further into our faith? Chapter 4 opens up some of the great questions of spirituality and considers the place of worship and prayer in sustaining the life of faith.

Finally, in Chapter 5, we draw the threads of the entire five volumes of the Christian Belief for Everyone series together as we think about how the Christian faith enables us to find truth, love and beauty, and pursue goodness. The American philosopher John Dewey (1859–1952) once declared that the 'deepest problem of modern life' is that we have failed to integrate our 'thoughts about the world' with our thoughts about 'value and purpose'.[1] He's right – all too often we fail to see the big picture because we focus on its individual components. We're so preoccupied with individual threads of our faith that we fail to see how they come together to disclose a pattern. In this final chapter we will weave together the multiple ideas we've developed in this series and see how they equip us to live out an authentic and meaningful life of faith.

Introduction

As before, I have great pleasure in dedicating this book to the people of the Shill Valley and Broadshire benefice in the diocese of Oxford, consisting of the churches in the Cotswold villages of Alvescot, Black Bourton, Broadwell, Broughton Poggs, Filkins, Holwell, Kelmscott, Kencot, Langford, Little Faringdon, Shilton and Westwell. This book, like the others in the series, is based on sermons I have preached in those village churches. For the purposes of this final volume I have incorporated two sermons preached in the chapel of Merton College, Oxford, and the parish church of Holy Trinity, Headington Quarry, Oxford.

Alister McGrath

1

The sacraments: signs and memories of hope

———•◆•———

I was giving a talk on the sacraments to a church audience back in the 1980s. They listened very politely to what I had to say – it was all standard textbook material. Yet I could tell that I wasn't really connecting with them. My attempts to explain the difference between a sign and what it signified weren't getting through. As I discovered afterwards, it wasn't so much that they couldn't understand me; they just couldn't see the point of what I was saying.

After ten minutes I abandoned my script and told them the story of an old aunt of mine who died some years ago. She had never married. After her death we found a battered old photograph of a young man in her bedside table. It turned out that my aunt had fallen hopelessly in love as a young woman. The love affair had ended tragically. She never found anyone else, and kept a photograph of the man she had loved for the remainder of her life. It was a sign of *something*, a point of contact with *someone*, who gave meaning to her life. The photograph was her only link with a lost and precious world in which she had been loved.

The audience came alive. They all knew people who kept things that reminded them of the past, and wanted to talk about them. In fact most of them did the same thing. These objects – photographs, signed books, pieces of jewellery and suchlike – connected them with people and events that really mattered to them. They were reassurances that they hadn't invented these memories. Remembering the past helped them cope with the present.

So I began to explain how my aunt's experience might help us grasp at least something of the importance of the sacraments. They were about more than just memories of the past; they were anticipations of our future. They connected our past, present and future. They reassured us of the foundations of our faith and gave us hope for the future. Afterwards many in the audience told me how much they enjoyed the talk – apart from the 'boring bit' at the beginning, of course.

Some readers will find it difficult to think about the sacraments. For a start the word is unfamiliar to many. In fact neither the New Testament nor the creeds make any mention of the specific word 'sacrament'. So why has a chapter in this book been given over to thinking about the sacraments when they seem to be of such little importance to the creeds? And as if that wasn't enough, Christians disagree fundamentally about the number, names and functions of the sacraments. How many are there? What should they be called? What do they actually do?[1]

Now these are all fair points, but it would be unthinkable to write a series of books about Christian belief without dealing with the place of the sacraments in the life of faith. They are a regular part of the life of faith of most Christians. Let's begin by asking how that strange word 'sacrament' came to be used and how we can make sense of it.

What is a sacrament?

Christians use the word 'sacrament' to refer to certain acts of worship that are understood to possess special importance in maintaining and developing the Christian life. At its heart a sacrament is a visible sign and reassurance of God's grace. These are not signs of our own devising; rather they have been entrusted to us and we are meant to use them. Our term 'sacrament' comes from the Latin word *sacramentum*, which originally meant 'a sacred oath', such as the oath of obedience a Roman soldier might swear to the people and Senate of Rome.[2] The third-century theologian Tertullian used this analogy to bring out the importance of sacraments in relation to Christian commitment and loyalty within the Church. Baptism, for example, can be seen as a sign both of allegiance to Jesus of Nazareth and of commitment to the Christian community.

The old Prayer Book catechism (1662) tells us that a sacrament is 'an outward and visible sign of an inward and spiritual grace given unto us, ordained by Christ himself, as a means whereby we receive the same, and a pledge to assure us thereof'. It's a great starting point, but more remains to be said. As I noted above, Christians are unable to agree on what sacraments are, what they should be called and what they do. Yet we must not see this as indicating incoherence in the idea of a sacrament! Rather it shows how we all find something in the sacraments that is special to us as individuals, which touches on our deepest hopes and fears. Each of us needs to sort out for ourselves what we make of them and how we work them into our own life of faith. This chapter aims to provide you with a toolkit to help you do that.

Sacraments are widely regarded as signs of God's promises. Augustine of Hippo was one of many early Christian writers who argued that the defining characteristic of a sacrament was that it was a sign of certain sacred realities: 'Signs, when applied to divine things, are called sacraments.' Yet he was clear that these signs were not arbitrary, in that there was some connection between the sign itself and what is being represented: 'If sacraments did not bear some resemblance to the things of which they are the sacraments, they would not be sacraments at all.' For example, baptism involves water, which is a sign of cleansing or purification – thus pointing to the cleansing and purification of the human soul through the grace of Christ. And bread and wine are both sources of nourishment – a reminder of the need for the believer to feed on Jesus of Nazareth as the 'bread of life'.

Yet sacraments are more than signs of spiritual realities; they are also an important corrective to our natural tendency to think of the life of faith in purely spiritual terms. C. S. Lewis is one of many writers to emphasize that, since we live in a material world, we should not be surprised that God chooses to use material things as a means of deepening our faith.

> There is no good trying to be more spiritual than God. God never meant man to be a purely spiritual creature. That is why He uses material things like bread and wine to put the new life into us. We may think this rather crude and unspiritual. God does not: He invented eating. He likes matter. He invented it.[3]

For Lewis, sacraments are material, visible and tangible things of this world that are able to help us grow in our faith and reinforce our belief in another world.

Some Christians worry that the material world can distract us from spiritual concerns. Is there not a risk, they wonder, that the physical world can draw us away from God? Perhaps – but it doesn't have to. After all, God created this world, and there are signs of God's presence within it. And more than that: God valued this world so much that he chose to enter it and redeem it from within.

This point was debated in the early Church. The movement known as Gnosticism regarded matter as evil and saw salvation in terms of deliverance from the material world. Yet Christian writers such as Irenaeus of Lyons were critical of this view.[4] John of Damascus (*c*.646–749) pointed out that the core theme of the incarnation was that God entered into the material world. God really became flesh – not some kind of spiritual phantasm or ghost. So how could the material world be opposed to the spiritual world, if God chose to inhabit that world in material form? Material objects – such as books and icons – could help us think more clearly about God.

Of course the world can, if we allow it, lead us away from God. But if we engage with the world properly it can deepen our appreciation of God as its creator. Think of Psalm 19, which speaks of the heavens declaring the glory of the Lord. This and many other biblical texts remind us that if we see the world in the right way it can enhance and enrich our grasp of the beauty and glory of God.

John Calvin developed a similar line of argument. For Calvin, a sacrament is 'an external sign, by which the Lord seals on our consciences his promises of goodwill toward us, in order to sustain the weakness of our faith'.[5] The sacraments are physical reminders and reassurances of God's promises, given to us precisely because God knows our weaknesses:

'Sacraments are a kind of seal of the promises of God.' The sacraments are given in material form because we need physical reminders of God's spiritual promises. Calvin cites with approval John Chrysostom's comments about our need to have 'spiritual things under things visible'.

These are good points but there's more that needs to be said. The important thing is this: the world can lead us *away* from God – but it can equally well lead us *to* God. In my own case, I came to faith partly by realizing that the beauty and ordering of the world, which I knew and appreciated as a scientist, pointed towards God – not away from God! C. S. Lewis used to think that immersing himself in books would ensure he stayed an atheist; then he discovered how many of the best books actually challenged atheism![6] So it is with the material world. Some say it's complete in itself but others – like myself – are clear that the material world itself leads us to believe that it is incomplete and that it points towards a transcendent reality that lies beyond it.

So how do sacraments help us in the life of faith? Let's begin our reflections by thinking about one of their functions, which is to help us to remember the great acts of God in the past and anticipate being with God in the future.

Remembering and anticipating: a central biblical theme

Remember! This theme resonates throughout the history of the people of God. They are to remember who they are. They are to remember how they came into being. They are to remember the words and deeds of the creator and saviour God who has called them and remains their comforter and guide to this day.

Everyone knows how important it is to keep memories alive. One of the best ways of preserving important memories is to tell stories. We've already seen how writers such as C. S. Lewis recognized that 'grand narratives' – such as the Christian story – help us to make sense of reality. Many anthropologists would agree.

> [We] are animals who must fundamentally understand what reality is, who we are, and how we ought to live by locating ourselves within the larger narratives and metanarratives that we hear and tell, and that constitute what is for us real and significant.[7]

But stories also help us to remember people and events that lie in the past yet are important to shaping and maintaining our identity as individuals and as communities. Sacraments remind us of the fundamental stories of the Christian faith – above all the exodus from Egypt and entry into the Promised Land, and the death and Resurrection of Jesus of Nazareth. Those are the stories that shape our identity and help us make sense of the world.

For many years I had a deep interest in the history of Switzerland, particularly during the fifteenth and sixteenth centuries. Switzerland came into being as a confederation of small territories – known as cantons – seeking independence from the rule of neighbouring Austria. A decisive moment in the history of the Swiss Confederation took place in April 1388 at the Battle of Näfels, in which a small group of soldiers from the three original cantons – Glarus, Uri and Schwyz – defeated a much larger Austrian army. So important was this victory for the survival of Switzerland that it is still celebrated through an annual pilgrimage to the battle site on the first Thursday in April. It became seen as a foundational event in the history of the nation. This pilgrimage was about both *remembering* an event and *grasping* its ongoing importance.

Objects also help us remember people and events. That's why we keep photographs of family members and friends. I have an old brass microscope on my office desk, given to me by my great-uncle in the early 1960s. He was a pathologist at the Royal Victoria Hospital in Belfast and wanted to encourage my growing interest in science. That microscope reminds me of my early love of the natural world, which led me to yearn to become a scientist. But it also reminds me of my great-uncle, who died a few years after he gave it to me. I expect most readers of this book can point to something that plays a similar role in their lives.

Objects come to have associations. They are linked to memories, people, aspirations, dashed hopes and turning points in our lives. Yet very often these associations are *personal* – the link between the object and a memory are known only to a few people. There are relatively few objects that have *public* associations – such as being linked with national memories or hopes. A good example of this is the use of poppies in Britain to recall the suffering and trauma of the First World War. The scarlet corn poppy was one of the few plants that was able to grow on the disturbed soil of the shell-cratered battlefields of Western Europe. In 1921 it was adopted as a symbol by the British Legion, responsible for caring for those who had been wounded in the war. It was a reminder of that war, and a symbol of commitment to those who were still affected by it – those who were wounded and those who had lost close relatives and friends in the conflict.

One of the greatest stories ever told concerns how the people of Israel were delivered from their harsh bondage in Egypt and led through the wilderness into the Promised Land of Canaan. It was a formative era for Israel, during which she had to learn the privileges and responsibilities of being the people of God. During this period Israel was able to reflect on the nature and character of her God. It led to the renewal of a sense of identity as the people of God.

The Passover celebration was about remembering the exodus, and became a focus for Israel's memory of its past and hopes for its future. When future generations asked why the Passover was being celebrated, they would be told about the deeper meaning of the event (Exodus 12.26–27). The Passover ritual recalled the history of the exodus from Egypt. Each household was to sacrifice an unblemished male lamb and brush some of its blood on its door frames as a mark of identity. The families would then roast the lamb and eat it, accompanied by bitter herbs and unleavened bread. The distinctively Christian idea of Jesus of Nazareth as the 'Lamb of God' reflects this theme, linking the death of Jesus on the cross with the Passover lamb.[8] So what was the point of this Passover ritual?

The Passover reminded Israel of the great events in history that brought her into being and gave her a specific identity that marked her out from all other peoples. The festival of Passover was to be a permanent memorial of the mighty acts of God that led to Israel being liberated from bondage in Egypt: 'Remember this day on which you came out of Egypt, out of the house of slavery, because the LORD brought you out from there by strength of hand' (Exodus 13.3). Once Israel had settled in the Promised Land she was to continue the Passover celebration as a way of remembering this act of divine deliverance.

Israel spent 40 years in the wilderness of Sinai, journeying from Egypt to the Promised Land. This long period of wandering in the wilderness was seen as a time of preparation. At some points it was a time of doubt, rebellion and restlessness, at others a time of dedication and purification – a period in which Israel was able to rediscover her identity as a people and the reasons for her being called into existence by the Lord.

So the Passover was an act of remembrance and anticipation. As Israel journeyed through the Sinai desert she looked *backwards* to the past, recalling her period of captivity in Egypt and her glorious liberation through Moses. She also looked *forwards* to the final entry into the Promised Land, the eagerly awaited goal of the long journey. The uncertainties and difficulties of the present were thus sustained by the memory of past events and the hope of future ones.

The themes of remembering and anticipating thus played a pivotal role in sustaining the people of Israel in the period between the exodus and the entry into Canaan. Israel was constantly reminded to remember her exile in Egypt and recall all that God had done for her since then (Psalms 135.5–14; 136.1–26).

A similar theme emerges during the captivity of the people of Jerusalem in Babylon during the sixth century before Christ. After Jerusalem fell to Babylonian armies in 597 BC, much of its population was deported to Babylon. Although some inhabitants remained in Jerusalem and the surrounding region, many of the most prominent Judaean families were deported in several waves into captivity in Babylon. Solomon's Temple, widely seen as the emblem of Jewish identity, was destroyed. The Jewish exiles in Babylon were left with no hope of returning to their homeland. The familiar words of

Psalm 137 capture the sense of longing felt by those exiles for their distant homeland: 'By the rivers of Babylon – there we sat down and there we wept when we remembered Zion.'

The thought of returning to their homeland sustained the exiles throughout the long and harsh years. They remembered Jerusalem and looked forward to returning to their homeland – even though they had no idea when this might happen, if at all. After the final defeat of Babylon by Persian armies in 539 BC the people of Jerusalem were free to return home. Although some chose to stay in Babylon, others undertook the long walk back to Jerusalem, to rebuild the Temple and reconstruct their national and religious identity.[9] The Old Testament books of Ezra and Nehemiah deal with this formative period in Israel's history, and help us understand the close interconnection of the rebuilding of the Jerusalem Temple and Israel's recovered sense of identity as the people of God.[10]

Thus far we have explored how sacraments interlink memory of the past and anticipation of the future. So how does this work out in practice? Let's explore this further. We'll begin by thinking about baptism.

Baptism: water and the life of faith

One of the great themes of the history of Israel is that its people were marked by a covenant sign – in this case, circumcision. This was a physical reminder of the relation of God and Israel. It was, of course, limited to males – women did not bear a sign of the covenant. That's why it's so important that the New Testament presents baptism as the sign of the 'new covenant' between God and all believers, irrespective of gender, bringing to fulfilment the 'old covenant' between God and Israel. This covenant sign of belonging to the people of God affirmed the fundamental equality of men and women before God: 'There is no longer Jew or Greek, there is no longer slave or free, there is no longer male and female; for all of you are one in Christ Jesus' (Galatians 3.28).

The Christian use of baptism can be traced back to Jesus of Nazareth's decision to be baptized by John the Baptist, described in the Gospels. Some find this puzzling. After all, the Nicene Creed speaks of acknowledging 'one baptism for the forgiveness of sins'. Surely Jesus did not have sins that needed to be forgiven? The point here, however, is that Jesus was baptized by John, who saw baptism as a sign of humanity's need for purification from sin. In being baptized, Jesus was both affirming the need of humanity for redemption and hinting that he himself would provide the basis for the real forgiveness of real sins.

Christians disagree about whether baptism causes forgiveness or is a public declaration that forgiveness has already been received and accepted. Yet all agree that, in some way, baptism is a means of reaffirming the reality of God's forgiveness of sins in Jesus of Nazareth, and of the human need for that forgiveness in the first place. Baptism affirms that our sins need to be washed away – and can be washed away – on account of the death and resurrection of Jesus. The symbolism of water is very powerful here, reminding us of water's ability to wash away stains and dirt, leaving us clean.

Yet there is another point here. Baptism is about connecting up our own individual stories with that of Jesus of Nazareth. It's a theme that we can see in Paul's important comments on baptism.

Do you not know that all of us who have been baptized into Christ Jesus were baptized into his death? Therefore we have been buried with him by baptism into death, so that, just as Christ was raised from the dead by the glory of the Father, so we too might walk in newness of life. For if we have been united with him in a death like his, we will certainly be united with him in a resurrection like his.

(Romans 6.3–5)

Through faith, we are united with Jesus. *His* story becomes *our* story. We will share in his death, just as we hope to share in his resurrection.

Yet the symbolism of baptism goes further than this. Early church writers pointed out how baptism was a reminder of the exodus from Egypt. Tertullian, a third-century writer, made this point as follows: 'The people of Israel, having been set free from bondage, escaped the violence of the Egyptian king by crossing over through water. Furthermore, it was water that destroyed the king himself, with his entire forces.'[11]

Baptism is thus a reminder of this great act of redemption, which is seen as prefiguring the greater act of redemption achieved through the death and resurrection of Jesus of Nazareth. Many Christians see baptism as more than a reminder of God's past faithfulness and activity, in some way effecting what it signifies. Martin Luther is a good representative of this position, as can be seen from his comments on baptism in his *Shorter Catechism* (1529):[12]

Q. *What gifts or benefits does Baptism bring?*
A. It brings about the forgiveness of sins, saves us from death and the devil, and grants eternal blessedness to all who believe, as the Word and promise of God declare.

13

Q. *How can water bring about such a great thing?*
A. Water does not; but it is the Word of God with and
through the water, and our faith which trusts in the Word
of God in the water. For without the Word of God, that
water is nothing but water, and there is no Baptism. But
when it is linked with the Word of God, it is a Baptism,
that is, a gracious water of life, and a bath of new birth
in the Holy Spirit.

As we have seen, one major aspect of baptism is its emphasis
on the continuity between the Church and the exodus of
Israel from Egypt. This continuity with the exodus is also
affirmed in the Eucharist, to which we now turn.

Bread and wine:
remembering and anticipating

As we have seen, the journey of faith is sustained by *memory*
on the one hand and *anticipation* on the other. During her
period of wandering in the wilderness of Sinai, Israel looked
back to her deliverance from Egypt and remembered the
faithfulness of the God who had called her into being. She
also looked ahead with an eager hope to the final entry into
the land that flowed with milk and honey. As Israel struggled
through the wilderness, these were anchors that secured her
faith in times of doubt. And there were times of doubt, when
some wanted to return to the safety and security of Egypt,
fearing uncertainty about their future.

Living between the times, poised in the present in that most
delicate interplay of past and future, was no easy matter for
Israel, and it remains challenging for Christians today. It
is like a trapeze artist who lets go of the security of one bar
and soars through the air, poised to catch the next support.

Each of the trapeze bars offers security, yet for a moment the artist is not supported by anything – she is suspended in an act of faith. The Christian life on earth is like those mid-air moments – moments of uncertainty and risk, which are only finally resolved when we take hold of what lies ahead of us and grasp it securely and irreversibly.

Christians are invited to remember and anticipate, allowing the past and the future to break into our present life of faith and enwrap it – just as, say, an alpine valley is enfolded by the mountains on either side. In the past we remember the great act of redemption in which God delivered us from sin, death and despair through the cross and resurrection of Jesus of Nazareth. And in the future we anticipate our final entry into the new Jerusalem to be with God for ever and find safety and peace in the presence of the risen Christ. The Christian life is framed by this memory and hope.

God's love is demonstrated in God's actions. To speak of the love of God is also to speak of the deeds of God that demonstrate, confirm and embody that love. Remembering and reflecting on God's past actions thus enables us to appreciate that faithfulness and trust in it in the future. The God to whom both Old and New Testaments bear witness is the same God with whom we have to deal today. *Remembering what God has done allows us to anticipate what God will do.* That's why Christianity can never simply be about remembering the past – it is also about anticipating the future.

To explore this further we are going to reflect on the place of the bread and wine in the Eucharist. But before we can do this we need to note two problems. First, there are disagreements over the name by which this sacrament is known; second, there are marked divergences between Christians concerning how it is to be understood. Let's begin by looking at four of the most common names Christians use to refer to the sacrament that focuses on the bread and wine.

The Eucharist This term is widely used in Greek-speaking Christianity and has also found general – though not universal – acceptance in the West. The basic meaning of the Greek word *eucharistia* is 'a giving thanks' or 'thanksgiving'.

The Mass This term is widely used within Catholicism and beyond. Its basic meaning is 'a dismissal', referring to the sending out of the congregation into the world after the service is completed. Gradually the name for this specific aspect of the service came to be applied to the service as a whole.

Holy Communion This name for the sacrament reflects the basic Christian conviction that it enables or encourages a deeper fellowship or 'communion' between the believer and Christ.

The Lord's Supper This term reflects the belief that the fundamental purpose of the sacrament is to recall the Last Supper – a pivotal moment in the life of Jesus of Nazareth, immediately preceding his betrayal, arrest, trial and crucifixion (Matthew 26.17–30; Mark 14.12–26; Luke 22.7–39).

So what does this sacrament do? Let's tease out some of its elements. First and most obviously, it is about remembering something that happened in the past – the Last Supper, in which Jesus of Nazareth broke bread and drank wine with his inmost group of disciples.[13]

> While they were eating, Jesus took a loaf of bread, and after blessing it he broke it, gave it to the disciples, and said, 'Take, eat; this is my body.' Then he took a cup, and after giving

thanks he gave it to them, saying, 'Drink from it, all of you; for this is my blood of the covenant, which is poured out for many for the forgiveness of sins. I tell you, I will never again drink of this fruit of the vine until that day when I drink it new with you in my Father's kingdom.'

(Matthew 26.26–29)

Paul's letters in the New Testament make it clear that the first Christians maintained this practice, seeing it as something they were commanded to do in memory of Jesus of Nazareth:

For I received from the Lord what I also handed on to you, that the Lord Jesus on the night when he was betrayed took a loaf of bread, and when he had given thanks, he broke it and said, 'This is my body that is for you. Do this in remembrance of me.' In the same way he took the cup also, after supper, saying, 'This cup is the new covenant in my blood. Do this, as often as you drink it, in remembrance of me.'

(1 Corinthians 11.23–25)

Notice how the Eucharist is depicted as an *action* that evokes a foundational memory of faith.

Yet this memory goes back much further. Three of the four Gospels – Matthew, Mark and Luke – represent the Last Supper as a Passover meal. Why is this so important? Because this means that the Last Supper was a meal in which Jesus and his disciples recalled the exodus from Egypt, reaffirming their links with a past act of divine deliverance – which Jesus would subsequently extend and enrich through his death and resurrection. At several points in the New Testament, Jesus is linked with the Passover lamb. For example, John the Baptist proclaims Jesus to be 'the lamb of God' (John 1.29), and Peter links the Passover lamb with Jesus, whom he describes as a 'lamb without blemish or defect' (Exodus 12.5; 1 Peter 1.19).

Despite these rich historical memories and associations, the Eucharist also looks forward. Celebrating the Lord's Supper on earth is to be seen as an anticipation of being present at the 'marriage supper of the Lamb' (Revelation 19.6–9). Believers are invited to look backwards to the foundational events of their faith and to look forward to their final consummation in the new Jerusalem. These ideas are developed in many Christian writings, such as Charles Wesley's famous hymn, 'Where Shall My Wondering Soul Begin?' The second verse of this hymn develops the idea that the Lord's Supper provides reassurance of the forgiveness of sins, and acts as an anticipation or foretaste ('antepast') of heaven.

> O how shall I the goodness tell,
> Father, which Thou to me hast showed?
> That I, a child of wrath and hell,
> I should be called a child of God,
> Should know, should feel my sins forgiven,
> Blessed with this antepast of Heaven!

Earlier in this section we noted some of the disagreements within the Christian churches over the significance of the bread and wine. We now need to consider these further.

Controversies: debates about the 'real presence'

As we have seen, there has been considerable debate within the Christian community over both the identity and function of sacraments, as well as what to call them.

Protestants generally accept only two sacraments – baptism and the Eucharist – where Catholicism and Orthodoxy recognize seven. The seven sacraments of the Catholic Church are generally grouped together in three categories: the sacraments of initiation (baptism, confirmation and the Eucharist), the sacraments of healing (reconciliation or penance, and the anointing or 'unction' of the sick) and sacraments of vocation (marriage and ordination). The Orthodox Church also recognizes these seven sacraments, while using the term 'chrismation' in place of confirmation.

These debates extend beyond the question of the number and names of the sacraments. One of the most important debates centres on the idea of the 'real presence'. The Gospels tell us that Jesus of Nazareth spoke these words as he broke the bread in the presence of his disciples: 'this is my body' (Matthew 26.26). But what are we to understand by these words? Many Christians see them as pointing to the bread becoming (or at the very least symbolizing) the body of Jesus of Nazareth, just as the wine becomes (or represents) his blood. In this section we will look at three positions within the Christian tradition on this question – not because we are going to resolve this discussion but because it will be helpful to have an idea of what the options are in thinking this through.

The doctrine of the real presence is grounded in the basic idea that the eucharistic bread and the wine are either transformed into the body and blood of Christ or represent him in such an efficacious manner that he may be regarded as present. The words spoken by Jesus of Nazareth over the bread at the Last Supper, and repeated in the liturgy of the Church, were clearly of foundational importance in relation to the emergence of this idea. It was therefore inevitable and entirely proper that considerable theological attention should be given to the explanation of the meaning of this practice. What did it achieve? And in what way did the eucharistic bread and wine differ from ordinary bread and wine?

In what follows we shall consider three main approaches to such questions that have been significant in theological debates. I leave it to my readers to decide which of them seems most appropriate or helpful. In each case I will provide the technical terms by which these positions are known, and then explain what they mean.

Transubstantiation

This approach is widely accepted within Catholicism, and holds that the bread and wine in the Eucharist really become the body and blood of Jesus of Nazareth. At the Last Supper, Jesus referred to the bread as his body (Matthew 26.26). Surely, many argued, this could only mean that the bread became the body of Christ? 'Transubstantiation' means 'a change in substance' and is derived from the Greek philosopher Aristotle's distinction between 'substance' and 'accident': the substance of something is its essential nature whereas its accidents are its outward appearances. The doctrine of transubstantiation holds that the accidents of the bread and wine (that is, their outward appearance, taste, smell and so forth) remain unchanged at the moment of their consecration, while their substance (that is, their inner identity) changes from that of bread and wine to that of the body and blood of Jesus.

This approach was reaffirmed by the Council of Trent in the sixteenth century, in response to Protestant criticisms: 'After the consecration of the bread and wine, our Lord Jesus Christ is truly, really, and substantially contained in the venerable sacrament of the holy eucharist under the appearance of those physical things.'[14] The Council vigorously defended both the doctrine and the terminology of transubstantiation.

> By the consecration of the bread and wine a change is brought about of the whole substance of the bread into the substance of the body of Christ and of the whole substance of the wine into the blood of Christ. This change the holy Catholic Church properly and appropriately calls transubstantiation.[15]

So why does not the appearance of the bread and wine change? The great medieval theologian Thomas Aquinas had an answer to this question.[16]

> It is obvious to our senses that after consecration all the accidents of bread and wine remain. And, by divine providence, there is a good reason for this. It is not normal for people to eat human flesh and to drink human blood; in fact, they are revolted by this idea. Therefore Christ's flesh and blood are set before us to be taken under the appearances of those things which are in frequent use, namely bread and wine.

Sacramental union or consubstantiation

A second view is especially associated with Martin Luther, and is characteristic of much contemporary Lutheran theology. Luther disliked the idea of transubstantiation, which seemed to him to be an attempt to rationalize a mystery. For Luther, the crucial point was that the risen Jesus of Nazareth was really present at the Eucharist – not some particular theory of the nature of that presence. The bread and the wine remained present but were supplemented – not replaced – by the presence of the risen Christ.

Luther borrowed an image from the patristic writer Origen to help him make his point: if iron is placed in a fire and heated, it glows – and in that glowing iron, both the iron and heat are present. Why not use some simple everyday analogy such as this to illustrate the mystery of the presence of Christ at the Eucharist, instead of rationalizing it using scholastic subtlety? It is not the doctrine of transubstantiation that is to be believed, but simply that Christ really is present at the Eucharist. It is more important to affirm this fact than to offer any theory or explanation of it.

This is reflected in the contemporary Lutheran belief that Christ's true body and blood are present in, with and under the external elements of bread and wine – even though this must be recognized as a divine mystery beyond human comprehension or explanation. This approach insists upon the simultaneous presence of both bread and the body of Christ at one and the same time. There is no change in substance; the substance of both bread and the body of Christ are present together, like iron and heat in the analogy just noted. In the same way, the substance of the wine and the blood of Christ are also present together.

Memorialism

For some Protestant writers, particularly within evangelical traditions, Christ is remembered in his absence at the Lord's Supper. The intellectual roots of this approach are often identified as lying in the writings of the Swiss Protestant theologian Huldrych Zwingli. Zwingli argued that the words spoken by Jesus of Nazareth at the Last Supper – 'this is my body' – should not be interpreted as equating the bread with the body of Jesus. Rather, they should be taken to mean that the bread represented or signified the body of Jesus. Zwingli argued that the Bible employed many figures of speech. Thus the word 'is' might at one point mean 'is absolutely identical with' and at another 'represents' or 'signifies'. The bread and wine were thus memorials of the crucifixion, reminders of the breaking of Christ's body and the shedding of his blood on Calvary.

Zwingli pointed out that both Scripture and the creeds affirm that Jesus of Nazareth is now 'seated at the right hand of God'. Now Zwingli has not the slightest idea where this might be, and wastes no time speculating on its location – but, he argues, it does mean that wherever Jesus is now, he cannot be present in the Eucharist. How could he be in two places at once? For this reason Zwingli proposes a doctrine of what we might call the 'real absence' of Christ at the Eucharist. Christ, who is somewhere else, is remembered in his absence, and the hope of his future return is reaffirmed. For Zwingli, the Eucharist was primarily about proclaiming 'the Lord's death until he comes' (1 Corinthians 11.26).

We have ended this section by noting how Christians diverge in their understanding of the sacraments. What I have tried to do is map out the main positions that Christians adopt on these questions, without endorsing any of them. My concern here is not to tell you what to think but help you to develop your own understanding of the place of the sacraments in the Christian life. Some of you, however, will want to know what I think on these questions, and I'm happy to tell you, providing you realize that these are just my ideas and that I'm not claiming any special significance for them.

It seems to me that the simple framework of 'remembering and anticipating' is a good starting point for thinking about the role of the sacraments. We recall what God has done in the past and we anticipate our future hope. In the case of the Eucharist, which plays a very important role in my own life of faith, I find myself being challenged to recall and enter into the great events of the past on which my faith is grounded – primarily the life, death and resurrection of Jesus of Nazareth, but also the exodus from Egypt.

I am also invited to look upwards in confidence and hope (not arrogance and complacency!), anticipating finally being able to see God – but this time no longer through a glass, darkly. God's faithfulness in the past reassures us of God's faithfulness in the future. These two anchors give me stability in the present. Now I am more than ready to concede that there is more to the sacraments than what I find in them – I'm simply saying what I find helpful in my own life of faith! That's what the journey of faith is all about – deepening our appreciation and grasp of the things of faith.

In the next two chapters we shall consider this Christian hope in greater detail, beginning with the all-important idea of the resurrection of the dead.

2

The resurrection of the dead

The creeds tell the Christian story, setting out the great themes and events on which our faith is based. They say that every good story keeps the best bits till the end, building up to a climax that weaves together everything that went before. Maybe that's what we find in the creeds! The Apostles' Creed reaches its climax in affirming our belief in 'the resurrection of the body, and the life everlasting'. The Nicene Creed speaks confidently of 'looking for' – of expecting, in the strong sense of the word – 'the resurrection of the dead, and the life of the world to come'. So what do these ideas mean? Why are they so important? And how do they feed into the life of faith, nourishing and sustaining us as we travel?

In *Lord and Saviour* we considered how the resurrection of Jesus helps unlock the mystery of his identity and significance.[1] Our understanding of who Jesus is and why he matters so enormously is shaped by his resurrection from the dead. The resurrection is one more piece in the theological jigsaw that discloses the bigger picture of the true identity of Jesus of Nazareth and the nature and purposes of God. Yet many readers will rightly point out that the resurrection of Jesus is important for believers as well. We believe that Jesus rose from the dead and that we shall one day be with him. The English poet George Herbert

(1593–1633) expresses this idea rather nicely in his famous poem 'Easter'.

> Rise, heart, thy Lord is risen. Sing his praise
> Without delays,
> Who takes thee by the hand, that thou likewise
> With him mayst rise.[2]

So what does Herbert mean by his powerful image of Christ taking believers 'by the hand', so that we may rise with him? In this chapter we shall explore some of the key themes of the Christian belief in 'the resurrection of the dead'.[3]

Resurrection and the universality of Jesus of Nazareth

When I was an atheist, I found myself puzzled by some of the things that Christian friends said about their faith. One of them spoke about having a 'relationship' with Jesus. This made no sense to me. I could understand how you could have a relationship with another human being – or even a cat or dog – but how could you relate to someone who was dead and you had never known in person? I asked him to explain what he meant by it: it was all, it seemed, about the importance of the 'resurrection'. Now this made it even more puzzling to me – something I couldn't understand was being explained by something I couldn't believe!

Now, of course, it does make sense to me – once I had got my mind around what Christianity was all about. The Gospels describe many encounters between Jesus of Nazareth and ordinary people, and the transformation this brought to the lives of tired, confused, rejected and wounded individuals. Someone like myself, who all too often thinks of the Christian faith primarily in terms of ideas, is challenged by these passages, which remind us that the Christian faith is about personal transformation through an encounter with Jesus. A good example of this is the encounter between Jesus and the first disciples by the shore of Lake Galilee (Mark 1.16–20) or his encounter with Zacchaeus (Luke 19.1–10).

Yet the New Testament does not limit such encounters to the period of the earthly life of Jesus of Nazareth. The risen Christ encounters individuals, transforming their personal worlds in doing so. The resurrection of Jesus broke down any barriers limiting him to any specific historical place or time. The incarnation is about God entering and inhabiting a slice of history; the resurrection is about Jesus transcending the limits of history and geography. The 'road to Emmaus' narrative is a classic example of this kind of encounter, in which two disciples find their worlds turned upside down as a result of their encounter with the risen Christ, whom they initially fail to recognize.

One of the most dramatic illustrations of this capacity of the risen Christ to encounter those who never knew him 'according to the flesh' is the 'conversion of Paul'. According to the New Testament, Saul of Tarsus was a Pharisee who was involved in early Jewish attempts to suppress Christianity. Paul himself relates that he was a Jew who was born at Tarsus in Cilicia (Acts 21.39). His father was a Roman citizen (Acts 22.26–28) and his family appears to have been religiously observant (2 Timothy 1.3). Paul was inclined to accept Pharisaic traditions and observances (Philippians 3.5–6). It is very difficult to date any aspect of his career with any certainty, including the famous journey to Damascus during which he experienced the presence of the risen Christ.[4]

We possess four accounts of this pivotal event. Three of them are found in the Acts of the Apostles. The first of these (9.1–19) takes the form of a straightforward narrative of events, whereas the second two (22.4–16; 26.9–19) form the core of Paul's self-defence before Jews in Jerusalem and King Agrippa respectively. A fourth account is found in one of Paul's earliest writings – the letter to the Galatians (Galatians 1.11–24). This version of the story does not go into historical detail but emphasizes that Paul saw his conversion as representing a calling from God to proclaim Jesus of Nazareth to the Gentiles. This account emphasizes his independence from the other apostles, all of whom knew Jesus during his lifetime.

So what happened? Let's look at the first account in Acts. At its heart we find an encounter between Saul of Tarsus and the risen Christ. While journeying with an escort to the city of Damascus to search for Christians to arrest, Paul experienced a moment of devastating illumination. 'A light from heaven flashed around him' (Acts 9.3), leading to his being thrown to the ground and blinded. Many scholars believe that this points to a moment of divine epiphany, in which the overwhelming glory of God was temporarily and dramatically revealed. Others have seen a connection with passages in the Old Testament that speak of the need for personal transformation and renewal using imagery very similar to that which we find in this famous story: 'The LORD will afflict you with madness, blindness, and confusion of mind; you shall grope about at noon as blind people grope in darkness' (Deuteronomy 28.28–29).

The emphasis on light recalls the first Genesis creation account with its dramatic declaration: 'Let there be light.' There may well be an anticipation here in Acts of Paul's famous declaration that 'if anyone is in Christ, there is a new creation' (2 Corinthians 5.17). The New Testament often uses the language of 'being born again' or 'being made new' in describing the difference made by an encounter with Christ, likening this transformation to a new birth. Paul's language is still more dramatic, envisaging a person's transformation through Christ as an extension of the work of creation itself.

Traditionally this episode is described as a conversion. There is undoubtedly some truth in this, in that Paul was changed dramatically from being the Church's main persecutor to one of its most important advocates in the Gentile world. Yet at another level it might be more helpful to see this as a calling rather than a conversion, similar to that of Samuel or one of the great Old Testament prophets. We see hints of this idea in some of Paul's letters, which speak of Paul being 'set apart' (Galatians 1.15–16) before he was born and called through grace. Paul would often appeal to his encounter with the risen Christ as the ultimate validation of his ministry.

Now while Paul's conversion story helps us understand how his ministry began and developed, it is also important in another way. It helps us grasp the deeper significance of the resurrection of Jesus. Why? Because it points to the removal of all spatial and chronological limitations to the scope of the risen Christ's action in the world. To put this another way: during his earthly ministry Jesus of Nazareth could only be encountered by individuals in the region of Judaea and for a period of about three years; after the resurrection Jesus could be encountered by all in any place and at any time – the limiting boundaries of history and geography have been transcended. Paul's experience parallels that of countless others who have had similar experiences down the centuries.

Yet Paul's experience went beyond his personal turnabout; it also led to a major revision in his way of conceiving God's dealings with the world – and above all, with the Gentiles. For Paul, the resurrection of Jesus of Nazareth clinched the arguments for his being the long-awaited Messiah, the one who would fulfil the hopes and aspirations of Israel. Jesus 'was descended from David according to the flesh and was declared to be Son of God with power according to the spirit of holiness by resurrection from the dead' (Romans 1.3–4). God, by raising Jesus from the dead, had proclaimed that he was indeed the true Messiah, the culmination and fulfilment of Israel's law and destiny. All people could be 'sons of God' through the new order – which Christians quickly began to describe as a 'new covenant' – that God has established through the resurrection.

The encounter between Saul of Tarsus and the risen Jesus of Nazareth on the road to Damascus thus involved both personal and intellectual transformation on Saul's part. Saul becomes a new person – a 'new creation' with a changed identity (seen in his new name) and a changed set of beliefs. Something similar can be seen happening in the remarkable case of the 'recommissioning' of the apostle Peter, to which we now turn.

Resurrection and recommissioning: the case of Peter

All of us fail from time to time – I certainly do. Where do I start? It's no accident that many of us find that failure leads to some kind of spiritual renaissance. We realize we've been trusting too much in our own strength and resources, and neglecting God. Sometimes a failure helps us reconnect with God and start rebuilding our lives. Instead of seeing failure as marking the end of our careers or lives, we see it as a wake-up call. It can help us learn and become better and stronger people.

There are so many stories that could be told to make this point. One of the most familiar is the conversion of Charles Colson (1931–2012).[5] Colson was a ruthless political operator who played a leading role in the White House under President Richard Nixon, when he became known as 'Nixon's hatchet man'. Then the Watergate scandal broke, and Colson was at its heart. His fall from power and influence was spectacular. Then he read C. S. Lewis's *Mere Christianity*, and was moved to tears by the chapter on the 'Great Sin'. He saw himself in Lewis's prose, and broke down. He was jailed for his part in the Watergate conspiracy. On being released he went on to found Prison Fellowship, one of the most important ministries to prisoners. Failure caused Colson to review and rethink, and opened the door to a new way of life and thought.

That's a pattern we see in the Gospel accounts of the betrayal, arrest and trial of Jesus of Nazareth. The Gospels depict Peter with ruthless honesty as a man with weaknesses who fails to live up to his aspirations. As Jesus and his disciples were walking towards the Mount of Olives after the Last Supper, Jesus told them they would all abandon him (Mark 14.27–31). Peter would have nothing of this. The other disciples might fail Jesus, but he wouldn't: 'Even though all become deserters, I will not.' Jesus seems to have known Peter rather better than he did himself: 'Truly I tell you, this day, this very night, before the cock crows twice, you will deny me three times.'

It's very easy for us to feel at least some sympathy for Peter, who clearly believes passionately that he will never abandon

Jesus, no matter how bad things get. Yet as subsequent events make clear, he simply could not cope with the pressure. While warming himself by a fire in the courtyard of the high priest after the arrest of Jesus, Peter found himself confronted by a servant-girl, one of the least significant people in the household of the high priest. Yet despite all his boasting about his bravery and commitment, in the end Peter proves unable to cope with what most of us would regard as a very modest threat – not from an armed soldier but from a servant-girl.

> While Peter was below in the courtyard, one of the servant-girls of the high priest came by. When she saw Peter warming himself, she stared at him and said, 'You also were with Jesus, the man from Nazareth.' But he denied it, saying, 'I do not know or understand what you are talking about.' And he went out into the forecourt. Then the cock crowed. And the servant-girl, on seeing him, began again to say to the bystanders, 'This man is one of them.' But again he denied it. Then after a little while the bystanders again said to Peter, 'Certainly you are one of them; for you are a Galilean.' But he began to curse, and he swore an oath, 'I do not know this man you are talking about.' At that moment the cock crowed for the second time. Then Peter remembered that Jesus had said to him, 'Before the cock crows twice, you will deny me three times.' And he broke down and wept. (Mark 14.66–72)

It is a moving story, one that rings true. It shows us how easily our aspirations crumble under pressure. Peter was reduced to tears by his own utter failure. Yet such moments of failure can be redemptive. They help us to see and confront our weakness, pride and arrogance. They allow us to realize the extent to which we have come to trust in our own strength and wisdom. When we fail, our personal weakness and frailty is exposed – sometimes only to ourselves but often in a more humiliating manner, to a wider audience. Charles Colson too was a broken and humiliated man, yet that turned out to be only half the story. He was also a man who would be transformed and renewed.

That's what grace is all about. There are times when Jesus of Nazareth has to break a hard heart, just as there are times when he heals a broken one. We see this happening here. Peter's failure did not mark the end of his ministry; it made possible a new beginning.

The encounter with the risen Jesus that led to Peter's restoration took place by Lake Galilee (otherwise known as 'the Sea of Tiberias' – John 21.1–19). Peter and the other disciples were standing by the shore. They had drifted back into their former occupations, becoming fishermen all over again. It had not been a good night for them. They had cast their nets throughout the night and caught nothing. Then a strange figure arrived on the shoreline: 'Just after daybreak, Jesus stood on the beach; but the disciples did not know that it was Jesus' (John 21.4). The stranger invites them to cast their net to the right-hand side of the boat. To their surprise, the nets are filled with fish. The incident calls to mind the first calling of the disciples in Luke's Gospel (Luke 5.2–10). The disciples were being recommissioned. And this renewal of their calling echoes the circumstances of their original calling to follow Jesus.

Yet the centrepiece of the story is Jesus' encounter with Peter. Jesus met Peter by the shore of the lake, standing by a fire on which some fish were cooking, with some bread near by. The fish and the bread called to mind – and were meant to call to mind – the feeding of the five thousand (John 6.5–15). Peter could hardly have failed to miss this powerful echo of the past. The fire would have evoked the memory of another fire, burning in the courtyard of the high priest, near which Peter had denied Jesus three times.

In the moving scene that follows, the risen Jesus offers Peter the opportunity to undo and turn his back on his failures in the past and begin all over again. Three times – once for each of his original denials – Jesus asks Peter whether he loves him. Peter clearly finds this a painful and distressing experience, yet insists on his love for Jesus in the face of this persistent questioning.

For each time that Peter reaffirms his love for the risen Jesus, he is offered and entrusted with a task – that of caring for the people of God. He is to feed Jesus' sheep and tend his flock. As if to bring home to Peter how costly this commission is going to be, Jesus hints at the manner of Peter's death. 'But when you grow old, you will stretch out your hands, and someone else will fasten a belt around you and take you where you do not wish to go' (John 21.18). Yet Peter will not fail Jesus again. According to a long-standing Christian tradition, Peter was crucified in the city of Rome during the reign of the emperor Nero, and asked to be crucified upside down since he was unworthy to be crucified in the same way as Jesus himself.

This narrative of a transformed and transfigured failure brings home one aspect of the resurrection hope that is too easily overlooked: the hope of personal transformation. We need to be reminded continually both of our failures on the one hand, to prevent us from becoming arrogant, and of the power and presence of the risen Jesus to renew us on the other, to prevent us lapsing into despair. The resurrection is indeed about hope – hope in the face of our future death but also in the face of our own failures and weaknesses.

The resurrection: a personal narrative of discovery

Dorothy L. Sayers remains one of our finest lay theologians. Time and time again she manages to express complicated theological ideas in simple and engaging terms. I often come back to her pithy comments about the importance of the resurrection of Jesus of Nazareth:

> One thing is certain: if [Jesus] was God and nothing else, His immortality means nothing to us; if He was man and no more, His death is no more important than yours or mine. But if He really was both God and man, then when the man Jesus died, God died too, and when the God Jesus rose from the dead, man rose too, because they were one and the same person.[6]

Sayers helps us to see that the identity of Jesus of Nazareth as true God and true human being establishes a connection between *his* resurrection and *ours*. As Paul points out, 'we suffer with him so that we may also be glorified with him' (Romans 8.17).

So what does this mean? Perhaps I could tell my own story of reflection and discovery here, as it may help others. My own conversion to Christianity was very rational. For me, the important thing was that Christianity was right – that it offered the best way (and certainly a better way than my earlier atheism) of making sense of what I saw in the world around me and experienced within me. I tended to trust my mind rather than my heart or imagination. I focused on *understanding* my faith, seeing the study of Christian ideas as being of central importance. At this stage I tended to see the resurrection as something that had really happened. I was more interested in affirming the historicity of the resurrection than working out what it meant for me personally.

Yet as I grew in faith I began to understand and appreciate how the Christian faith connects up with life at more profound levels than mere reason. A deeper appreciation of the significance of the resurrection slowly began to dawn. I had always understood that its significance went beyond deepening our understandings of the identity of Christ and of our own situation. Yet I found it difficult to express this in words and could not quite grasp its traction on the deeper things of life. If I could put this a little formally: my first years of faith saw me focusing on the rational merits of the resurrection, overlooking its existential implications.

The best testing ground for any theology is pastoral ministry. My appreciation of the deeper dimensions of the gospel grew considerably as I worked in a parish in the East Midlands in the early 1980s, ministering to those who were suffering, dying and bereaved. Ordinary people, often in the final stages of their life, explained to me how their faith in the resurrection transformed their lives and brought new hope to their sufferings and losses. As I listened to them, I realized that they were ministering to me as much as I was to them. They were opening my eyes to something I had overlooked.

What those good faithful Christian people taught me was that the resurrection enabled believers to do more than think. It helped them to *cope* with the sorrows, ambiguity and pain of life. They hadn't read the great theologians who had written tomes about the resurrection, such as Wolfhart Pannenberg (1928–2014). But they had immersed themselves in the New Testament and absorbed its fundamental message of hope. They knew that, even though they walked through the valley of the shadow of death, God was with them. So they kept on walking through the wilderness of this world, knowing God was by their side. They knew that Christ's resurrection was the firm foundation for their hope that all who trusted in him would finally rise with him and be with him in the new Jerusalem. So they faced suffering with dignity and serenity, knowing that those who suffer with Christ will be glorified with him.

To put it simply: ordinary Christian believers helped me realize that the resurrection changed the way we lived, not just the way we think. Things that I had understood in a rather dry and detached way now became living realities. What I had once studied, I now inhabited. What I had once understood, I now embraced. My time in a parish helped me realize that the gospel impacted on every aspect of our existence – our reasons, emotions, imaginations and values. Looking back on those days, I can now see that they liberated me from an impoverished view of the Christian faith. There's nothing wrong with a faith that shapes the way we think – as long as we allow it to do its work of transformation on every aspect of our lives. The healing balm of the gospel needs to salve the wounds of every faculty that we possess, so that they can all be transformed, enriched and empowered through the grace of God.

The resurrection is about more than an historical event. It is about more than an unveiling of the true significance and identity of Jesus of Nazareth. It is also about the birth of a justified hope that all of us who trust and follow Jesus will one day be with him, where he has gone before us to prepare a place for us. Belief in the resurrection throws open the door to a hopeful and purposeful way of living in which we know that, whatever life may throw at us, we can trust in the constant presence and love of God as our shepherd, and look forward to being with him for ever.

Living in the shadow of the cross

One of my favourite accounts of the importance of the crucifixion is Frederick Buechner's *Magnificent Defeat*. It's a collection of sermons originally published in 1966, and speaks powerfully of the deeper message of Christmas and Easter. What I appreciate particularly about this work is its beautiful use of language, which somehow manages to affirm the core doctrinal truths of the Christian faith while at the same time enabling them to saturate the imagination, allowing a new depth of engagement with these great themes of belief. If I had to identify one single signature quotation, it would be this:

> Remember Jesus of Nazareth, staggering on broken feet out of the tomb toward the Resurrection, bearing on his body the proud insignia of the defeat which is victory, the magnificent defeat of the human soul at the hands of God.[7]

You need to read that a few times to see the point, but it's powerful once you do. God's in charge. We may not fully see this – we may see a visible defeat that reduces us to despair. But that's not the true picture – there is a deeper truth, too easily overlooked, which is that this apparent human defeat is in truth a divine victory, which takes hold of us and supports us. 'Faith is stepping out into the unknown with nothing to guide us but a hand just beyond our grasp.'[8]

Buechner puts our dilemma as believers like this: '"Lord, I believe; help my unbelief" is the best any of us can do really, but thank God it is enough.'[9] We want slick and easy answers and all too often we don't get them. Sometimes we find our-selves to be spiritually bewildered and discouraged. That's why the cross is so important: it helps us to see our doubts and confusion in a new light.[10] The writer who helped me to grasp this point was Martin Luther (1483–1546). Let's see what Luther has to say on this – in what follows I'll para-phrase his ideas, framing them to bring out their importance for coping with the ambiguities of the life of faith.[11]

Luther develops a 'theology of the cross' that sees the image of the crucified Christ as the lens through which we must see our world of experience. The narrative of the crucifixion, suffering and death of Jesus of Nazareth is to be seen as the 'grand narrative' that helps us to make sense of, *and cope with*, the doubts and anxieties that assault us as we journey on the road of faith. So often it seems to us that the shadows overwhelm the light. Despite the 'big picture' that faith provides, we often struggle to make sense of some things, especially suffering. So what does Luther have to say that might help us wrestle with this enigma?

Luther asks us to reflect on the sense of helplessness and hopelessness that seems to have gripped the disciples at Calvary on that first Good Friday, as Jesus of Nazareth died upon the cross. The crowd who gathered around the cross were expecting something dramatic to happen. If Jesus really was the son of God, they could expect God to intervene and rescue him. Yet as that long day wore on, there was no sign of a dramatic divine intervention. In his cry from the cross even Jesus himself experienced a momentary yet pro-found sense of the absence of God, 'My God, my God, why have you forsaken me?' Many expected God to intervene dramatically in the situation, to deliver the dying Jesus, but nothing of the kind happened. Jesus suffered and finally died.

There was no sign of God acting in that situation, so those who based their thinking about God solely on experience drew the obvious conclusion: God was not there.

Now the resurrection revealed that God was very much present and active at Calvary, working out both the salvation of humanity and the vindication of Jesus of Nazareth. What experience interpreted as the *absence* of God, the resurrection demonstrated to be the *hidden presence* of God. God was active behind the scenes, working in secret. For Luther, the resurrection demonstrates how unreliable the verdict of human experience really is. Instead of relying upon the misleading impressions of human experience, we should trust in God's promises. God promises to be present with us, even in life's darkest hours.

Lots of movies have plotlines that explore a similar theme. Characters think nobody cares about them but in reality it turns out someone really loves them; they think they've been abandoned when in fact people are working to help them. Most people won't think of the 2004 film *Bridget Jones: The Edge of Reason*[12] as a theological movie, but those theological motifs are there if you know where to look. Remember the bit when Bridget Jones is thrown into a jail in Thailand and thinks she's been abandoned by her lawyer boyfriend? In fact, of course, the boyfriend – memorably played by Colin Firth – is working away to pull strings to get her set free. Bridget's sense of being alone and abandoned chimes in powerfully with the feeling many of us go through in times of doubt and anxiety. Yet in the end we need to trust God in these matters.

Luther suggests that we think of the life of faith as being like that first Good Friday. We see many things that puzzle and frighten us and lead us to conclude that God is absent from or inactive in that situation. Suffering is an excellent example. How, we often wonder, can God be present in human suffering? Much the same thoughts must have passed through the minds of those watching Jesus of Nazareth suffer and die. The first Easter Day, however, transformed that situation – and our understanding of the way God is present and active in his world. It showed that God is present and active in situations in which experience thinks he is absent and inactive – such as suffering.

God chose to be present in the darker and inevitable moments of life – such as pain, suffering and death. These are not areas of life from which God has been excluded but areas in which God has deliberately chosen to be present, even if we sometimes find that presence hard to experience. And for Luther – and for me! – that thought helps to keep us going as we walk through the shadow lands on our way to the new Jerusalem.

The shape of the heavenly body

The New Testament reassures us that we are 'citizens of heaven', but there's a nagging question that puzzles some of us: What do these citizens of heaven look like? The New Testament hints at such matters as a mystery rather than disclosing them as facts. The image of a seed, used by Paul in 1 Corinthians 15, clearly suggests that there is some organic connection between our earthly and heavenly bodies. Our resurrected bodies could be conceived as the unfolding of some potential that was built into human nature by God. The real theological issue here was to affirm the *continuity* of identity between our earthly and heavenly bodies, while at the same time insisting on their fundamental difference.

Paul's analogy of a seed unquestionably affirms this basic theme of 'continuity and development'.

Now some readers will protest at this point – rightly, I think. To worry about what we will look like in heaven seems pointless. The important thing is to know that we shall one day be in the presence of the living and loving God. Surely that's enough to keep us going! Why fuss about something that is both speculative and trivial? I'm with you on this one, yet I know from many conversations that some people want to think about these issues, however tentatively. So let's explore some options, bearing in mind that nobody really knows the answers and that we don't need to have them to live out a good Christian life!

One possibility would be to imagine the streets of the new Jerusalem as being inhabited by disembodied souls. This was the view taken by Origen, a third-century theologian who was influenced by Platonism. Origen held that the resurrection body was purely spiritual. As we saw in *The Spirit of Grace*, this reflects the Platonic idea that the human being consists of two entities – a physical body and a spiritual soul. Death leads to the liberation of the soul from its material body. This view was commonplace within the Hellenistic culture of the New Testament period. However, it was rejected by most early Christian theologians, who understood the phrase 'the resurrection of the body' as the permanent resurrection of both the body and the soul of the believer, not their separation.

So what would these resurrected individuals look like? Some early Christian writers argued that the 'citizens of heaven' would be naked, recreating the situation in the Garden of Eden. This time, however, nakedness would give rise to neither shame nor sexual lust, but would simply be accepted as the natural and innocent state of humanity. Others, however, suggested that the inhabitants of the new Jerusalem should be clothed in finery, reflecting their status as citizens of God's chosen city. It is an honour to be a citizen of such a great city; our clothing must surely reflect this new status.

There's another issue that worries many people, with good reason. What about those who are disfigured at the time of their death? Someone might die from the most hideous wounds in battle. Did that mean that their resurrected body would be similarly mutilated? Or what if someone lost an arm in an accident? Methodius of Olympus (died *c*.311) offered an analogy for this process of continuity and change that is helpful in reflecting on the question of disfigurement through disease or wounds. The resurrection could, Methodius suggested, be thought of as a kind of 'rearrangement' of the constituent elements of humanity. It is like a statue that is melted down and reforged from the same material – yet in such a manner that any defects or damage are eliminated. Let's follow through his analogy in a little more detail.

Methodius asks us to imagine a 'skilled artificer' who had cast a 'noble image' in gold or some other material. It was beautifully proportioned in all its features. Then, to his dismay, the artificer notices that someone has defaced the image because he was jealous of its beauty. So what is to be done? How is a damaged and defaced masterpiece to be restored? The craftsman decides he has only one solution: he will have to start all over again. He will melt 'this noble image' down again and recast it. Let's pick up Methodius's theological interpretation of his analogy.

> Now it seems to me that God's plan was much the same as this human example. He saw that humanity, his most wonderful

creation, had been corrupted by envy and treachery. Such was his love for humanity that he could not allow it to continue in this condition, remaining faulty and deficient for ever. For this reason, God dissolved humanity once more into its original materials, so that it could be remodelled in such a way that all its defects could be eliminated and disappear. Now the melting down of a statue corresponds to the death and dissolution of the human body, and the remoulding of the material to the resurrection after death.[13]

A similar argument is found in the *Four Books of the Sentences*, the educational masterpiece of the great twelfth-century theologian Peter Lombard. This book, which served as the core textbook for just about every medieval theologian, took the view that the resurrected body was basically a reconstituted humanity, from which all defects had been purged.

A new debate arose in the twentieth century when the practice of cremation became increasingly common in Christian nations, partly on account of the rising cost of burial, raising the question of whether cremation was inconsistent with belief in the resurrection. The issue emerged as theologically significant during a persecution of Christians in Lyons around the years 175–7. Aware that Christians professed belief in the 'resurrection of the body', their pagan oppressors burned the bodies of the Christians they had just martyred and threw their ashes in the River Rhône. This, they believed, would prevent the resurrection of these martyrs, in that there was now no body to be raised. Christian theologians responded by arguing that God was able to restore all that the body had lost through this process of destruction.

Perhaps the most influential answer to this question about cremation was offered by the famous American evangelist

Billy Graham. In a series of articles, Graham noted that many Christians were uneasy about the practice of cremation because it involved the total annihilation of the body. Yet surely, he argued, this same issue arose with the practice of burial. After all, the graves of our ancestors are no longer in existence. For Graham, it was clear that what happens to the body or to the grave cannot be of any significance so far as the resurrection is concerned. In fact 'the Bible does not give specific directions for the disposal of the body following death'.[14] Graham thus endorsed cremation as acceptable to Christians, as it posed no threat to the hope of resurrection.

> At the resurrection it will not make any difference whether a person's body has been buried or cremated. God knows how to raise the body, either in the resurrection of life or the resurrection of condemnation (John 5.28–29). The new body of a Christian will be a radically changed and glorified body like the body of the exalted Christ. It will be an eternal, spiritual body never again to experience weakness, disease, suffering, or death (1 Corinthians 15.35–54 and Philippians 3.20–21).[15]

There's one more question that we need to think about – though again, some readers will find this pointlessly speculative. If someone dies at the age of 90, will they appear in the streets of the new Jerusalem in the form of an old person? Or if someone dies at the age of five, will they appear as a child? This issue caused the spilling of much theological ink, especially during the Middle Ages. By the end of the thirteenth century an emerging consensus can be discerned. As each person reaches their peak of perfection around the age of 30, they will be resurrected as they would have appeared at that time – even if they never lived to reach that age.

Peter Lombard's twelfth-century discussion of the matter is typical of his age: 'A boy who dies immediately after being born will be resurrected in that form which he would have had if he had lived to the age of thirty.' Honorius of Autun (1080–1154) made much the same point a century later: 'All the dead – an infant of one year as much as a man of ninety – will rise with the same age and size as Christ when he rose, namely, thirty years old.' The great Franciscan theologian Bonaventure of Bagnoregio (*c*.1217–74) argued that the physical status of Jesus at the time of his death was normative for the resurrection body: 'Perfect grace conforms us to Christ our head, in whom there was … perfect age, due stature, and fair appearance.' All physical blemishes and impediments are healed or removed through the resurrection.

> Those who died in childhood will be raised by divine power at an age corresponding to that of Christ at his resurrection (although not with exactly the same physical size). The old and emaciated will be restored to what they were at that age. Giants and dwarves will have their proper stature bestowed upon them. And so all shall come forth, whole and perfect, to the perfect humanity, to 'the measure of the full stature of Christ' (Ephesians 4.13).[16]

Now many will probably join me in feeling that this kind of speculation is interesting but ultimately a little pointless. Still, when I visit art galleries and look at medieval depictions of people in heaven, I can't help but notice that Peter Lombard's theological reflections seem to have been taken seriously by a lot of artists!

Let's move on, and think more about the Christian hope. What difference does this make to the way we think and live?

3

Heaven and eternity: the Christian hope

———•◦•———

Back in the 1960s I was drawn to Marxism. Why? I think there were two reasons. One of them was that Marxism offered a big picture of reality, which I found intellectually exciting. The philosopher Mary Midgley suggests that Marxism – one of the 'great secular faiths of our day' – is a 'large-scale, ambitious system of thought' that displays 'religious-looking features'.[1] I admired the depth of its engagement with reality. It was only later that I discovered that Christianity rivalled it in terms of its ability to offer an intelligible and coherent account of reality.

The other thing that attracted me to Marxism was its no-nonsense insistence that we ought to engage with our world and make it a better place. Karl Marx talked about religion as the 'opium of the people', meaning that it dulled people's interest in doing something about changing the world. A belief in another world after death, he argued, distracted people from engaging with this world, here and now. At the time, I thought he was right. Now I think he failed to grasp the all-important point that the Christian vision of heaven gives us both a template and a motivation to change this world. If heaven is a place where there is no more suffering, why should we not try and make earth more like heaven? When rightly understood, the Christian conception of heaven is actually a stimulus to social action, medical research and relief work. As C. S. Lewis wrote, 'The Christians who did most for the present world were just those who thought most of the next.'[2]

But let's begin our reflections in this chapter by looking at the question of whether heaven is just a delusion. We've touched on some of these themes earlier in this series, but they merit reconsideration.

Heaven: too good to be true?

I come from a medical family. When I was growing up I would occasionally hear my father and his friends talking about 'snake oil'. It sounded wonderfully mysterious, and I assumed it was some exotic kind of medicine. What did it do, I wondered? Well, I soon found out: nothing. My father and his colleagues were using the phrase to refer to patent medicines that made completely unrealistic promises – promises people wanted to believe in the hope of being healed from chronic illness. These patent medicines played on people's fears, giving false hopes on the one hand and reduced bank balances on the other. I suppose that as I grew older and became a hardened atheist, it was natural that I would think of religion in the same way: it was an exploitative delusion.

By the age of sixteen I was a grumpy and frankly rather arrogant atheist, totally convinced there was no God and that anyone who thought there was needed to be locked up for their own good. Religion was a delusion. At that stage I was concentrating on the study of the natural sciences and had won a scholarship to Oxford University to study chemistry, beginning in October 1971. I had every reason to believe that studying the sciences further would confirm my rampant godlessness. While waiting to go up to Oxford I decided to work my way through a pile of improving books. Needless to say, none of them were religious. All the same, some of them planted the seeds of doubt in my mind.

I often wonder what would have happened to me had I read some words of C. S. Lewis when I was eighteen years old and been alerted to the danger of reading: 'A young man who wishes to remain a sound Atheist cannot be too careful of his reading. There are traps everywhere.'[3] Maybe I would have avoided books unless they had been approved by leading atheists as 'sound'. But my curiosity knew no bounds, and I read voraciously. Eventually I came to a classic work of philosophy – Plato's *Republic*. I couldn't make sense of everything I read, but one image etched itself into my imagination. Plato asks us to imagine a group of men trapped in a cave, knowing only a world of flickering shadows cast by a fire. Having experience of no other world, they assume that the shadows are the only reality. Yet the reader knows – and is meant to know – that there is another world beyond the cave, awaiting discovery.

As I read this passage, the hard-nosed rationalist within me smiled condescendingly: typical escapist superstition! What you see is what you get, and that's the end of the matter. Yet a still, small voice within me whispered words of doubt. What if the world we observe and experience is only part of the story? What if this world is only a shadow land of something better and greater? What if there is something more wonderful beyond it? Wasn't that what Christians meant when they talked about heaven?

I hadn't read Joseph Addison's famous remarks about Plato then. Addison (1672–1719) was a noted eighteenth-century poet and journalist who knew a sense of transcendence within human experience that pointed towards God.[4]

> Plato, thou reason'st well!
> Else whence this pleasing hope, this fond desire,
> This longing after immortality?

For Addison, this was no delusion, no wishful thinking invented to console humanity in the midst of a meaningless universe. The sense of transcendence so many people knew and experienced was sent from heaven, and was meant to lead to heaven.

> 'Tis heaven itself, that points out an hereafter,
> And intimates eternity to man.
> Eternity! thou pleasing, dreadful thought!

Neither had I read Lewis's remarkable account of his growing realization of the imaginative deficiency of his youthful atheism. I've cited this line from *Surprised by Joy* before in this series but it's always worth repeating: 'On the one side, a many-islanded sea of poetry and myth; on the other, a glib and shallow rationalism.' Yet even without Lewis, a seed of doubt had been planted within my dogmatic mindset. I could not have known this, but within a year such doubts would overwhelm me and lead me to rediscover Christianity.

Perhaps one of the biggest problems I had with Christianity as a young man was that the notion of heaven seemed both pointless and ridiculous. I took particular offence at a line of poetry by Robert Browning that I came across: 'God's in His heaven – All's right with the world!' This spoke of a distant God, safely cocooned in a remote region, isolated from the pain and suffering of our world. I had yet to grasp the fundamental idea of the incarnation, so memorably stated by G. K. Chesterton: 'God left his heavens precisely in order to set the world right.'[5]

It's a great thought – but some readers will still have concerns. Isn't this idea of heaven just too good to be true? Isn't it a bit like the 'snake oil' I mentioned earlier? Now we're right to be sceptical here. We want to be able to check things out. We want to know we haven't chosen to build our lives on a fiction, on delusions or lies – even though they may be, as Lewis again put it, 'lies breathed through silver'. Let's look briefly at some of the concerns that can trouble people.

One concern sometimes raised is about the historicity of the resurrection: it was just what people of that day and age expected. It was easy to believe in the resurrection 2,000 years ago – but not today. Yet it's not that straightforward. First-century Judaism had many beliefs about the resurrection.[6] Most thought of a general resurrection as something that would happen in the distant future, when God would finally raise all people at the end of time. Others – such as the Sadducees – denied even this idea altogether. Paul, of course, was able to exploit these differences between Jewish religious parties in his debates (Acts 23.6–8). Yet it's important to realize that no Jewish authority thought in terms of the resurrection of a human being here and now. Resurrection was a distant hope.

Nor was it clear that the resurrection of Jesus of Nazareth would have been seen as a sign of hope by everyone. Some at the time would have seen this as unsettling, a cause for fear rather than hope. The idea of resurrection was easily misunderstood in terms of dead people returning to life. The idea of the dead returning to the land of the living was seen as deeply threatening, especially in Roman pagan thought. The dead were safely confined to a shadowy world from which they could never return to haunt the living. The realization that Jesus had broken free from the bonds of death would have caused terror and amazement in about equal measure. And that is exactly how the Gospels portray initial reactions to this declaration. Mark's dramatic account of the women's discovery of the empty tomb does not end in joy, but fear (Mark 16.8).

One of those who believed that the resurrection was just too good to be true was the disciple we remember as 'Doubting Thomas'. The Gospels tell us frustratingly little about Thomas. The few statements directly attributed to him suggest that he was something of a hard-nosed realist, tinged with a world-weary pessimism. Thomas seems to have been traumatized by the death of Jesus on the cross. Unable to cope with that dreadful event and its possibly more dreadful implications, he slipped away from the others. He knew nothing of the resurrection appearances that so transformed the outlook of the other apostles. On hearing their accounts of the resurrection, he refused to believe them.

Why? Perhaps Thomas regarded these reports as incredible. He wanted proof. Or perhaps he had grown conscious of having become something of an outsider, set apart from the other disciples through not having shared their experience of the risen Jesus. Yet whatever the explanation for his doubts and hesitations, Thomas wanted reassurance. 'Unless I see the mark of the nails in his hands, and put my finger in the mark of the nails and my hand in his side, I will not believe' (John 20.25). And let's be honest here: many of us, in our heart of hearts, would have said the same. Thomas is a representative figure who helps us to bring our doubts and hesitations into the open.

It's good that someone voiced these doubts before us. And the reply Thomas received from the risen Jesus helps us connect with his anxieties and share in his subsequent reassurance: 'Have you believed because you have seen me? Blessed are those who have not seen and yet have come to believe' (John 20.29). That's why the Christian hope is so important. We anticipate more than being with God in the new Jerusalem: it's about finally knowing for sure that who and what we have trusted was indeed trustworthy.

So how are we meant to think about heaven? Perhaps this is the wrong question. Perhaps we ought to ask how we are meant to *visualize* heaven. The New Testament is more concerned with helping us to *see* heaven in our mind's eye than with understanding it through our reason. We are invited to grasp the reality of heaven through our imaginations, by reflecting on biblical images. Two of these are of especial importance: the image of a city and the image of an enclosed garden. In what follows we will explore these two images and consider how they illuminate our hope of heaven.

The new Jerusalem

'I saw the holy city, the new Jerusalem' (Revelation 21.2). These words from the final book of the Bible set out a vision of heaven that has long captivated the Christian imagination. To speak of heaven is to affirm that the human longing to *see* God will one day be fulfilled – that we shall finally be able to gaze upon the face of what Christianity affirms to be the most wondrous sight anyone can hope to behold. One of Israel's greatest Psalms asks to be granted the privilege of being able to gaze upon 'the beauty of the LORD' in the land of the living (Psalm 27.4) – to be able to catch a glimpse of the face of God in the midst of the ambiguities and sorrows of this life. We see God but dimly in this life; yet as Paul argued in his first letter to the Corinthian Christians, we shall one day see God 'face to face' (1 Corinthians 13.12).

The image of the 'new Jerusalem' has exercised a powerful influence over Christian literature and art down the centuries. It is found towards the end of the book of Revelation. This important and difficult work reflects the social exclusion or persecution faced by Christians in the later years of the reign of the Roman emperor Domitian, around the year 90.[7]

> Then I saw a new heaven and a new earth; for the first heaven and the first earth had passed away, and the sea was no more. And I saw the holy city, the new Jerusalem, coming down out of heaven from God, prepared as a bride adorned for her husband. And I heard a loud voice from the throne saying, 'See, the home of God is among mortals. He will dwell with them; they will be his peoples, and God himself will be with them; he will wipe every tear from their eyes. Death will be no more; mourning and crying and pain will be no more, for the first things have passed away.' And the one who was seated on the throne said, 'See, I am making all things new.' Also he said, 'Write this, for these words are trustworthy and true.'   (Revelation 21.1–5)

The consolation of heaven is here contrasted with the suffering, tragedy and pain of life on earth. The theme of the new Jerusalem is integrated with motifs drawn from the Genesis creation accounts (such as the presence of the 'tree of life' – Revelation 22.2), which suggests that heaven can be seen as the restoration of the bliss of Eden, when God dwelt with humanity in harmony. The pain, sorrow and evil of a fallen world have finally passed away; creation has been restored to its original intention.

The Christians of Asia Minor at this time were few in number and generally of low social status. There is no doubt that they derived a great deal of consolation from the anticipation of entering a heavenly city that vastly exceeded any earthly comforts or security they had known. The holy city was paved with gold and decked with jewels and precious stones, dazzling its inhabitants and intensifying the sense of longing to enter through its gates on the part of those still on earth.

There is no temple in the new Jerusalem (21.22). The old order has passed away. There is no longer any need for a priesthood or a temple. All are now priests, and God dwells in the midst of his people. Where the prophets of the Old Testament yearned for the rebuilding of the Temple, the book of Revelation declares that it has become redundant. What it foreshadowed has now come to pass.

This image of heaven resonates strongly with one of the leading themes of Paul's theology. He makes a distinction between those who 'set their minds on earthly things' and those whose citizenship is 'in heaven' (Philippians 3.19–21).[8] Paul was a Roman citizen, who knew what privileges this brought – particularly on those occasions when he found himself in conflict with the Roman authorities. For Paul, Christians possessed something greater: the citizenship of heaven, which is to be understood as a present possession, not something yet to come. While believers have yet to enter into the full possession of what this citizenship entails, they already possess that privilege. As the author of the letter to the Hebrews puts it, 'here we have no lasting city, but we are looking for the city that is to come' (Hebrews 13.14).

Paradise: heaven as an enclosed garden

Everyone knows about paradise. The word has come to have rich associations of peace, tranquillity and delight. We use it to refer to a blissful holiday island or a quiet sandy beach lit by a warm sun and washed by a turquoise sea. Yet the word has a deep resonance for Christians. Paradise is about heaven, where we live in the presence of a loving and living God. Jesus of Nazareth's words to one of the thieves who was being crucified with him have had a deep impact on Christians: 'Truly I tell you, today you will be with me in Paradise' (Luke 23.43).

So where does this word come from and what does it mean? It comes from the languages of the ancient Near East, including the Old Persian word *paradeida*, which probably designates 'an enclosed garden' or perhaps 'a royal park'.[9] The Greek word *paradeisos* – probably borrowed from the Persian original – is often used in the writings of historians such as Xenophon to refer to the great walled gardens of the royal palaces of Persian kings such as Cyrus.

The original garden, of course, was Eden, a place of fertility and harmony where humanity dwelt in peace with nature and 'walked with God'. While much popular literature speaks of the 'Garden of Eden', it is better to think of 'Eden' as the region in which the garden is located rather than the name of the garden itself. Other biblical passages designate the garden in other ways – such as the 'garden of God' (Ezekiel 28.13) or the 'garden of the LORD' (Isaiah 51.3). The garden came to be a symbol of lost innocence and harmony, a place of peace, rest and fertility. Although paradise was now lost, it could be restored.

Hosea, writing in the eighth century before Christ, looks forward to a future transformation of the human situation, in which human enmity against other humans is ended, along with a restoration of the integrity of the original created order (Hosea 2.18). A related theme can be seen in the writings of Joel, in which a series of paradisiacal images are fused with themes taken from the entry of Israel into the Promised Land.

> In that day the mountains shall drip sweet wine, the hills shall flow with milk, and all the stream beds of Judah shall flow with water; a fountain shall come forth from the house of the LORD and water the Wadi Shittim. (Joel 3.18)

Hints of the theme of paradise are found in the New Testament. One of the most important encounters with the risen Christ in John's Gospel took place in a garden (John 19.41). Mary Magdalene is reported as encountering the risen Christ, and initially believed that he was 'the gardener'. There is evidence that the term 'gardener' may have been used as a title for some ancient monarchs. Might Mary's initial belief that Jesus is the gardener be seen as a deeper recognition of the lordship of the risen Jesus over paradise?

The image of paradise as an enclosed garden was developed during the earliest stages in Christian history. Even as early as the second century, the walled garden was being interpreted as an image of the Christian Church. Irenaeus remarked that 'the Church has been planted as an enclosed garden [*paradisus*] in this world', and developed a rich and evocative account of the life of the Church on the assumption that it was a means of bearing and restoring the lost values of Eden to the world.

Interestingly, many medieval attempts to depict heaven merge the images of a city and garden, portraying heaven as a citadel surrounded by lush parklands, enclosed by walls. The walls are not there to keep the faithful inside; they are to protect them and offer them safety from whatever dangers may lie outside. Christian believers are depicted as citizens of heaven, with the right to reside within the safety of heaven, all threats and dangers having been removed. The close fellowship between God and humanity, so important a theme in the Genesis creation narratives, is now restored and renewed. That's why Cyprian asked Christians to remember, when they faced the threat of death from illness or persecution, that 'paradise is our native land'.

I've emphasized that the hope of heaven appeals to our imagination rather than our reason. So how do Christian writers with a deep sense of the importance of the imagination in grasping the deepest spiritual truths and insights respond to the hope of heaven? In what follows, we're going to look at two well-known writers who engage this theme – J. R. R. Tolkien and C. S. Lewis. Tolkien is the less explicitly Christian of these two writers, often wearing his faith lightly. But as we shall see, there are points in *The Lord of the Rings* where the theme of the hope of heaven shines through.

J. R. R. Tolkien on hope in a dark world

I was asked to preach at a special service at Merton College, Oxford, to mark its 750th anniversary in 2014. I was a Senior Scholar at Merton from 1976 to 1978, and was delighted to be asked back to my old college for this landmark event. It's always good to mark special occasions and think more deeply about their importance. In its long and distinguished history, Merton College has passed through times of light and darkness. The year 2014 also marked the centenary of the outbreak of the First World War, an event that called into question the all too easy assumption that human beings were essentially rational and good. Those four years of brutal conflict were a dark time for this Oxford college, as they were for the British nation and far beyond. How, many asked, could we keep going in such dark times? What hope is there that we can hold on to?

That need for hope remains important to all of us. At Christmas, many Christians return to a reading from the prophet Isaiah (Isaiah 40.1–8): 'Comfort, O comfort my people, says your God.' They are words familiar to many of us, not least because they open Handel's great oratorio *Messiah*, widely performed at this time of year. Those words speak to us today just as they spoke deeply to their original audience – the people of Jerusalem in exile in Babylon, far from their homeland. Would they ever return home? Those too were dark times. And in the midst of that darkness, Isaiah spoke words of comfort and hope. God had not forgotten his people – they would return home! That hope sustained them as they waited for their liberation. Yes, they were still in exile, but they had hope for the future.

We still need hope: not a naive and shallow optimism but a robust and secure confidence that there is something good – there is *someone* good – who will triumph over despair and hopelessness. Many felt the need for that hope during the First World War – including J. R. R. Tolkien, a Second Lieutenant in the Lancashire Fusiliers, who took part in the Battle of the Somme and went on to become a fellow of Merton College in 1945. Tolkien's epic work *The Lord of the Rings* was written and published during his time as Merton Professor of English at Oxford University.

The Lord of the Rings is now widely regarded as one of the great works of English literature. One of its most distinctive themes is the reality of evil. Tolkien names evil, thus giving us permission to challenge the bland and inadequate moral outlook of our age, which insists we respect everything. Like his close friend C. S. Lewis, Tolkien was convinced that we had lost the moral vocabulary that enabled us to speak of evil and thus to fight it.

But that is not the only theme we find so powerfully explored in Tolkien's epic work. It affirms the role of the weak and powerless in changing the world for the better. That's why Hobbits – such as Frodo Baggins and his sidekick Samwise Gamgee, also known as 'Sam' – are so important in the narrative of *The Lord of the Rings*. They are the little people, and in the end they are the ones who make the difference. They may feel they are part of a story that is too big for them, yet they grow to take up their places within it. It's easy to feel overwhelmed by a sense of despair and powerlessness as we contemplate a world we seem incapable of redirecting towards the good. Yet as Tolkien so clearly saw, we need a vision of the good and a sense of empowerment in the midst of our weakness if anything is to be changed.

Many feel that one of the most powerful themes affirmed by Tolkien is the reality of the Christian hope in the midst of despair and seeming helplessness. We see this especially in a narrative passage found towards the end of *The Lord of the Rings*, at a moment when the victory of the forces of darkness seems assured:

> There, peeping among the cloud-wrack above a dark tor high up in the mountains, Sam saw a white star twinkle for a while. The beauty of it smote his heart, as he looked up out of the forsaken land, and hope returned to him. For like a shaft,

clear and cold, the thought pierced him that in the end the
Shadow was only a small and passing thing: there was light
and high beauty for ever beyond its reach.[10]

Tolkien's subtle reworking of the imagery of the 'star of
Bethlehem' affirms the resilience of hope in God in the face
of a darkening world of fading human dreams. That's the
kind of hope that kept the people of Jerusalem going during
their time of exile. Their God was beyond the reach of human
tyranny and oppression, and one day things would change.
That's the hope that keeps many of us going as well – the
thought that there is something beyond this world of suffering and pain, which we will one day enter and embrace. It's
a theme we find so powerfully expressed in the New Testament's vision of the new Jerusalem, a world in which God
has made everything anew and there is no more sorrow, pain
or death.

But there is another theme in *The Lord of the Rings* that
speaks powerfully to us today as we reflect on the sobering
and harsh realities of a world darkened by terror and violence.
As the work nears its end, the victory of evil seems inevitable.
A dark mood settles over the narrative – and then everything
changes. An unexpected event enables the ring to be destroyed,
breaking the power of evil. Tolkien called this a *eucatastrophe* –
a dramatic, unexpected event that disrupts a narrative of
despair and redirects it towards the good.

For Tolkien, the best and greatest example of this radical
upheaval of a story of hopelessness is the resurrection of
Christ, a dramatic event that brought first astonishment
and then hope – a real hope, grounded in something and
someone trustworthy. That is the hope that is to be seized
and acted upon, which keeps us going and keeps us growing

even in the darkest of times. It is no accident that most of the events of *The Lord of the Rings* are set in what some scholars term the 'mythic space' between Christmas and Good Friday.[11] The Christian hope of heaven raises our horizons and elevates our expectations – inviting us to behave on earth in the light of this greater reality. The true believer is not someone who disengages with this world in order to focus on heaven but someone who tries to make this world more like heaven.

Tolkien – one of the twentieth century's most subtle Christian writers – needs to be heard here. One of the central themes of the Christian tradition is the need for a warranted hope in a faithful God in sustaining us and inspiring us: 'The grass withers, the flower fades; but the word of our God will stand forever' (Isaiah 40.8). That hope in God, like Sam's vision of 'light and high beauty', can never be taken away from us. The world around us is changing – and not for the better. Many of us feel that the optimism of an earlier generation has now receded. We are facing hard questions, difficult times, uncertainties about the future. But we must not despair. 'The word of our God will stand for ever' – and we will stand with it.

We have already noted the importance of the imagination in grasping the importance of the Christian idea of heaven. One of the twentieth century's most important Christian writers was noted for his appeal to the imagination in gaining a full appreciation of the Christian faith. So what does C. S. Lewis have to say about heaven?

C. S. Lewis on the hope of heaven

An American colleague visiting Oxford went to see Lewis's grave in the churchyard of Holy Trinity, Headington Quarry, on the outskirts of Oxford. Afterwards he came to visit me. Over a cup of tea we discussed the somewhat forbidding Shakespearean epitaph that adorns Lewis's gravestone: 'Men must endure their going hence.' My friend was puzzled. The inscription seemed to speak of a passive recognition of the inevitability of death. It was an affirmation of human mortality rather than a celebration of the hope of heaven. Wasn't Lewis meant to be a Christian? So why this melancholy motto, more suggestive of a defiant Stoicism than a joyful Christianity?

Now the text in question was actually chosen by Lewis's elder brother, Warren, who lived with Lewis in Oxford until his death. It had been the 'text for the day' on the family calendar for the day of their mother's death from cancer in 1908, when Lewis was nine years old.[12] Its grim realism came to express the views of the young Lewis, who became an aggressive atheist as a young man, especially when serving as an infantry officer in the First World War. Where was God in the midst of the carnage he saw all around him?

Yet this proved to be a passing phase, not a resting place. Lewis's gradual move away from atheism towards Christianity reflected his growing realization that atheism lacked real intellectual substance, and seemed imaginatively impoverished. Lewis had been haunted by a deep intuition that there had to be more to life than what his minimalist atheism allowed. Above all, he found himself reflecting on the implications of a deep and elusive sense of longing, which was heightened rather than satisfied by what he found around him.

Lewis famously termed this experience of yearning 'Joy', and came to the conclusion that it pointed to something beyond the boundaries of human knowledge and experience: 'If I find in myself a desire which no experience in this world can satisfy, the most probable explanation is that I was made for another world.'[13] A transcendent realm beyond us – what Christians call 'heaven' – would make sense of what he experienced within him and observed around him.

For Lewis, heaven was to be thought of as a realm beyond the limits of present human experience yet signposted by our deepest intuitions and experiences. It was like hearing the sound of music faintly, coming from across the distant hills, or catching the scent of a far-off flower, wafted by a passing breeze. Lewis came to see such experiences as 'arrows of Joy', a wake-up call to discover and experience a deeper vision of reality.

Many scholars think that Lewis's early vision of heaven was perhaps Platonic as much as it was Christian. It was a sense-making device – like Plato's world of ideals – that affirmed the coherence of the world of thought and experience. As Lewis himself put it at that time, 'It matters more that Heaven should exist than that we should ever get there.'[14]

Yet by the 1940s Lewis had embraced a deeper vision of heaven. While he never lost sight of the belief that the idea of heaven helps us make sense of what we experience and observe on earth, the hope of entering heaven and experiencing its joy became increasingly important to him. For Lewis, this world is God's world and is to be valued, appreciated and enjoyed. Yet it is studded with clues that it is not our real home; that there is a still better world beyond its frontiers; that we may dare to hope to enter and inhabit this better place.

Lewis affirms the delight, joy and purposefulness of this present life. Yet he asks us to realize that when this finally comes to an end, something even better awaits us. He believed that the secular world offers people only a hopeless end, and wanted them to see and grasp the endless hope of the

Christian faith and live in its light. Perhaps some words of Jewel the Unicorn in *The Last Battle*, the concluding novel of the Chronicles of Narnia series, capture this point particularly well: 'I have come home at last! This is my real country! I belong here. This is the land I have been looking for all my life, though I never knew it till now.'[15] For Lewis, the Christian hope is about returning home to where we really belong.

Does this mean that Lewis exults in death? Is he a 'world-denying' writer who treats this world as devoid of value? No. Lewis is clear that this is where we are meant to be – for the moment. Although we realize that this world is not our final destination, we know that we are meant to do more than just pass through it. We are called to make it a better place, so that it echoes the values and vision of heaven. Like countless spiritual writers before him, Lewis declares that the hope of heaven enables us to see this world in its true perspective. This life is the preparation for that greater realm – the title page of the Great Story.

So how does this way of thinking relate to the Christian story of the death and resurrection of Jesus of Nazareth? While Lewis's writings show him to have had a good grasp of basic Christian theological themes by 1940, his appreciation of their existential depth seems to have emerged later. His *Grief Observed* of 1961 incorporates the suffering of Christ on Good Friday into his reflections on his wife's slow and lingering death from cancer, leading him to a deeper grasp of the ability of the Christian faith to support people in times of bewilderment and suffering.

In much the same way, Lewis's later realization that he too was dying from cancer seems to have prompted a more profound reflection on the meaning of Christ's resurrection. In some of his letters in the final months of his illness, Lewis spoke of the hope that he had in the face of death. He was, he wrote, 'a seed waiting in the good earth: waiting to come up a flower in the Gardener's good time, up into the *real* world, the real waking'.[16] While Lewis's gravestone might speak of our shared mortality, his works and his witness point to something more profound – hope in a greater reality and a better realm, the door to which is thrown open by the death and resurrection of Jesus Christ.

As we saw, one of Lewis's most important insights concerns our feeling that there is more to life than what we see around us. In what follows, we'll explore this in more detail.

The lure of heaven

I love one of G. K. Chesterton's little aphorisms. 'We have come to the wrong star . . . That is what makes life at once so splendid and so strange. The true happiness is that we *don't* fit. We come from somewhere else. We have lost our way.'[17] The idea of heaven intrigues, consoles and inspires. And one of the reasons for this is that it chimes in with one of our deepest intuitions. This isn't our true home. We belong somewhere else. Our true destiny lies in another place. Maybe this world is a preparation for this greater realm, but it's not where we really belong.

In the previous chapter I mentioned Frederick Buechner's book *The Magnificent Defeat*. There's a sentence in that collection of sermons that fits perfectly into the line of thought we've been exploring.

> Like Adam, we have all lost Paradise; and yet we carry Paradise around inside of us in the form of a longing for, almost a memory of, a blessedness that is no more, or the dream of a blessedness that may someday be again.[18]

Read it twice! It's a wonderful synopsis of a core idea that we find in Augustine and so many others: that humanity has lost its paradise but we can never shake off its memory, which lingers as a sense of longing or hope. Maybe one day we can return to a restored paradise.

Intuitions like these can, of course, mislead us. But what if they can *inform* us? Christians don't see the hope of heaven as an invention, a consoling delusion for losers or a means of escape from the hopelessness of our world. It's there. And we catch snatches of its music in this world – as we are meant to.

Let's look at an example. On a May morning, possibly in 1362, a poet lay down on a grassy bank, close to England's Malvern Hills. He was already weary with wandering. The gentle babbling of the nearby brook and the soft radiance of the late spring sun soon made him drowsy, and he fell fast asleep. He 'began to dream a marvellous dream', in which he was transported from the harsh realities of fourteenth-century English life to another more wonderful realm, far removed from the war-ravaged, plague-ridden and politically corrupt England he knew. The vision of heaven set out in William Langland's famous dream, *Piers Plowman*, made a direct appeal to the deep human longing for something better than the world known to the senses.[19] Surely there must be more than this? The vision of heaven that so entranced Langland and his many readers proved to have the power to console those who feel overwhelmed by the sorrow and pain of this life. The great African-American spirituals of the 1860s – such as 'Swing Low, Sweet Chariot' – are a powerful and deeply moving witness to the intense consolation derived from dreaming and singing of a better life, which served both as an emotional compensation for present sufferings and grievances and a stimulus to hope for the future.

To those who feel overwhelmed by what D. H. Lawrence called 'the grey, gritty hopelessness of it all', the idea of heaven is as liberating as it is enticing. Might there not be another country beyond our vision, yet whose distant music we faintly hear in the depths of the night or whose fragrance is carried to us by a passing breeze, leaving us longing to know more of this far-off land? And might we even dare to hope to enter it? Western culture would be immeasurably impoverished without the imaginative stimulus that these lines of thought have provided to countless generations of poets, writers and thinkers.

George Herbert's important poem 'The Pulley' (1633) uses a mechanical analogy to explore the lingering sense of the divine within human experience, and indicate how it may be transformed. The poem draws extensively on a single biblical image for heaven – that of 'rest'. God, according to the Genesis creation accounts, 'rested' on the seventh day and ordained that humanity should also rest every seventh day as a Sabbath. This idea was developed within the Bible as an image of heaven, which finally provided the eternal 'rest' that had been promised to the people of God. The idea is developed with particular force in the letter to the Hebrews, which affirms that God has promised a 'rest' into which believers can hope to enter (Hebrews 4.2–10).[20]

The human longing for rest can thus be interpreted as a secret longing to enter into the promised rest of heaven, in which weary humans can 'rest from their labours' (Revelation 14.13). Herbert's basic premise here is that God has created humanity 'restless for heaven'; until that goal is achieved, humanity will remain unsatisfied and dislocated. The poem opens by affirming that in the creation of humanity, God bestowed all manner of blessings upon them, including

strength, beauty, wisdom, honour and pleasure. Yet one gift
was withheld – that of rest. God 'made a stay' – that is, held
back from giving humanity the gift that would have allowed
us to become completely self-sufficient and autonomous.
Herbert argues that the bestowal of the full complement of
gifts would have led to humanity adoring the gifts of God
rather than the God who had given them.

For Herbert, it is human exhaustion that moves us to
rediscover God rather than the mere taking pleasure in the
gifts of God. The human yearning for rest thus becomes the
engine that drives the human quest for God and the final
securing of rest in heaven.

> Yet let him keep the rest,
> But keep them with repining restlessness:
> Let him be rich and weary, that at least,
> If goodness lead him not, yet weariness
> May toss him to my breast.[21]

Some may judge Herbert to be cynical at this point. Yet
what he is saying is that many do, as a matter of fact, find
themselves turning back to God on account of an awareness
of the fleeting pleasure of the world. There has to be something more than this. The hope of heaven sometimes breaks
into our consciousness because we are drawn to it directly; as
Herbert knew so well, it sometimes gains an entrance because
we become so dissatisfied with its alternatives.

So how does this Christian vision of hope affect our lives?
What difference do these beliefs make to us as we make the
journey of faith? We have already noticed how Christianity
provides us with a map, which helps us journey through
the landscape of faith. How does it help us to live in hope?
In the next chapter we shall turn to consider some ways of

thinking that are helpful as we travel. The Christian 'map of reality' helps us to realize that we are sojourners and pilgrims here on earth, whose true home and destiny is the new Jerusalem. We can travel in faith and hope, knowing that our true destiny lies where the risen Jesus has gone before us. We'll explore these themes further in what follows.

4

Between the times: the life of faith

———•◆•———

There are some lines that I keep coming back to in Matthew Arnold's 'Stanzas from the Grande Chartreuse', written about 1850. Arnold speaks of himself as

> Wandering between two worlds, one dead,
> The other powerless to be born,
> With nowhere yet to rest my head . . .[1]

Arnold was caught up in the tension between a settled past world of faith and an unknown future in which faith might seem to be little more than a 'dead time's exploded dream'. The ancient monastery that prompted his thoughts seemed to belong to an alien world, something whose faith might be admired but was no longer shared. Arnold felt he did not really belong anywhere, caught up in the painful tension between a dead past and the uncertainties of the future.

Many Christians feel a similar tension in their lives. We seem to be suspended between two worlds – the world we now know and inhabit and the unseen world we believe we will one day enter. We are passing through one world, which is not our home, on our way to another, which is where we truly belong. We are sojourners and pilgrims here on earth, travelling to the new Jerusalem. We travel in faith and hope, believing that our true destiny lies in heaven, where the risen Jesus has gone before us.

So how do we sustain our faith as we travel? How do we avoid becoming so heavenly minded that we are no earthly use, or so locked into the affairs of the world that the hope of heaven is swamped by day-to-day concerns?

These are questions that Christian theologians and spiritual writers have engaged with down the ages,[2] and they are clearly important to the themes of this series. In this chapter we shall explore some of their ideas and see how we can make use of them. Let's begin by thinking more about the idea of the life of faith as a journey.

Journeying to heaven

How should we think about the Christian life? What images or analogies might be helpful? One that many have found valuable is the image of a journey. This has long been recognized as an important way of stimulating the Christian imagination and sustaining the hope of heaven.[3] Both the Old and New Testaments describe journeys undertaken by individuals or entire peoples, such as Abraham's journey to Canaan or Paul's great missionary journeys. Two journeys that have been particularly important for many Christians as they try to make sense of the life of faith should be noted here:

1 the 'wilderness wandering' of the people of Israel, which lasted for 40 years before they finally entered into the Promised Land;
2 the return home of the people of Jerusalem after decades of exile in the distant city of Babylon.

Each of these journeys has become an image of considerable importance for Christian spirituality, offering us a framework to make sense of our experience in the world and help us find our bearings as we travel. The Christian faith speaks of a journeying God – a God who accompanies us as we travel, who is there in moments of sorrow and joy, even when we pass through the valley of the shadow of death (Psalm 23).

A journey is about more than simply getting from one place to another; it is about becoming wiser and more resilient as we travel, not least because we make the journey of faith in company. For a start, we don't – and we're not meant to – journey on our own. As we saw in *The Spirit of Grace*, Christianity is a faith lived in community. Others hold us up and help us grow as we travel. We're not left on our own. The process of journeying makes us stronger and wiser.

The New Testament tells us that the early Christians initially referred to themselves as followers of 'the Way' (see, for example, Acts 9.2; 24.14). Just as God led the people of Israel out of captivity in Egypt into the Promised Land, so the Christian life can be seen as a slow process of deliverance from bondage to sin before being led triumphantly into the heavenly city.

At several points in the writings of St Paul the image of a journey is subtly transformed into that of a race – a long and arduous journey, undertaken under pressure, in which the winners receive a crown (see Galatians 2.2; 2 Timothy 4.7). The same image is also used in the letter to the Hebrews, which urges its readers to persevere in the race of life by keeping their eyes focused firmly on Jesus (Hebrews 12.1–2). This image stresses the importance of discipline in the Christian life, and the joy of completing the race and joining others who have already run their course, while encouraging others to keep going.

The theme of the hope of heaven, and especially the consummation of all things in the heavenly Jerusalem, is of major importance in Christian spirituality. The Latin term *viator* – literally, a 'wayfarer' – was widely used during the Middle Ages to refer to believers. This term invites us to see ourselves as pilgrims travelling to the heavenly city. The vision of the heavenly city is both an encouragement and inspiration as we travel. It's a helpful way of getting us to focus our attention on the hope of our final entry into the new Jerusalem and the rejoicing and delight this will bring. It helps us deal with disappointments and hardships as we travel.

The image of 'journeying to heaven' has a long history of use within the Christian tradition. The object of the Christian life is thus to arrive safely in the heavenly homeland. For this reason, many spiritual writers stress the importance of cultivating indifference to the world. In his sermon 'The Christian Pilgrim', Jonathan Edwards (1703–58) stresses the importance of focusing on the hope of heaven:

> God is the highest good of the reasonable creature, and the enjoyment of him is the only happiness with which our souls can be satisfied. — To go to heaven fully to enjoy God, is *infinitely* better than the most pleasant accommodations here. Fathers and mothers, husbands, wives, children, or the company of earthly friends, are but shadows. But the enjoyment of God is the substance. These are but scattered beams, but God is the sun. These are but streams, but God is the fountain. These are but drops, but God is the ocean.[4]

Now Edwards is not in any way disparaging the world as God's good creation. Nor does he suggest that Christians ought to disengage from the world, as if it were of no importance. His concern here is that Christians might come to value the creation more highly than the creator, and as a result settle for something that is good, but not as good as God. Yet Edwards is clear that focusing on heaven inspires us to serve in the world. It may not be our final goal or the place where we really belong; yet it is where we have been placed by God and where we are called to serve God.

C. S. Lewis made a similar point in his reflections on heaven. Having emphasized that the thought of heaven galvanizes us into social action, he makes the further point that we need to do all that we can to sustain our hope of heaven, and pass this on to others:

> I must take care, on the one hand, never to despise, or be unthankful for, these earthly blessings, and on the other, never to mistake them for the something else of which they are only a kind of copy, or echo, or mirage. I must keep alive in myself the desire for my true country, which I shall not find till after death; I must never let it get snowed under or turned aside; I must make it the main object of life to press on to that other country and to help others to do the same.[5]

For Lewis and others, the vision of heaven as a place in which there is no pain and suffering is an inspiration to us. We can try and make this world through which we are travelling more like heaven – that's one of the reasons so many Christians see medical work as a way of living out their calling in the world.

The image of journeying from our place of exile to our 'true country' captivated the imaginations of many, especially when this was framed in terms of travelling from the 'city of this world' to the 'heavenly city'. In what follows we shall look at two of the best-known representatives of this way of thinking and ask what we can learn from them.

Augustine and John Bunyan
on the 'Two Cities'

Augustine of Hippo's influential work *The City of God* was written at a time when the settled world order of his age had been plunged into uncertainty. The great city of Rome had been sacked by the barbarians in 410. The Roman Empire seemed on the point of collapse, marking the end of the stable political and social world of late antiquity. In *The City of God*, Augustine set out to explore the tension between the instability and uncertainty of the 'now' and the hope of the 'not yet'. He developed the image of the 'two cities' as a mental map to help Christians make sense of this situation and cope with the anxiety and unease they felt.

A central theme of *The City of God* is the relation between two cities – the 'city of God' and the 'secular city' or the 'city of the world'.[6] The Christian life takes place between the coming of Jesus of Nazareth into the world and his final return in glory. The Church is a community of people who are in exile in the 'city of the world'. It is *in* the world yet not *of* the world. There is a tension between the present reality, in which the Church is exiled in the world and tries to maintain its distinctive identity in the midst of a hostile world, and the future hope, in which it will be delivered from the world and finally allowed to share in the glory of God. Believers are saved, purified and perfected – in hope but not yet in reality. For Augustine, believers are able to reach out in hope, beyond their present condition. This is not a spurious or invented hope but a sure and certain one grounded in the resurrection of Christ.

The image of the 'two cities' is developed in a somewhat different way in John Bunyan's classic work *The Pilgrim's*

Progress. Bunyan (1626–88), one of the best-known Puritan writers of the seventeenth century, became involved with the Puritan cause during the English Civil War (1642–51). With the establishment of the Puritan Commonwealth of England in 1649, Bunyan turned his attention to preaching and became the minister of an independent congregation in Bedford. His Puritan sympathies caused him to be out of favour when the English monarchy was restored in 1660, with the result that he spent many years inside Bedford jail. Bunyan used his time in prison to write his autobiography, *Grace Abounding to the Chief of Sinners*, and begin work on his best-known work, *The Pilgrim's Progress*, the first part of which appeared in 1678 and the second in 1684.[7]

The Pilgrim's Progress can be read as both an adventure story and an allegory of the struggles, temptations, sufferings and final salvation of the human soul. The story of the book focuses on its hero, Christian, initially bowed down with a burden of sin upon his back, who flees from the City of Destruction and seeks eternal life. He thus sets out on a long and arduous pilgrimage, which leads him from the mire of the Slough of Despond up the straight and narrow path of the Hill of Difficulty, down into the Valley of Humiliation – where he battles with the foul fiend Apollyon – and into the terrifying Valley of the Shadow of Death. He passes through Vanity Fair with all its worldly allurements, is held captive by Giant Despair in Doubting Castle and at last, after crossing the bridgeless River of Death, is received in the Celestial Jerusalem.

Although the Christian life had been portrayed as a pilgrimage long before Bunyan, there are no reasons for thinking that he knew or used these previous discussions in his own writing. *The Pilgrim's Progress* is best regarded as a brilliant and highly original narrative, incorporating biblical ideas and imagery without the mediating filter of previous writers. The only literary source that may be identified with any certainty is the King James translation of the Bible, which appeared in 1611 and is known to have had a deep impact on the shaping of the imagery and vocabulary of modern English.

Like Augustine in *The City of God*, Bunyan uses the journey from the City of Destruction to the heavenly city as a framework for making sense of the ambiguities, sorrows and pains of the Christian life. His powerful appeal to imagery, coupled with a masterly use of narrative, ensured that the imagery of the new Jerusalem would have a profound and permanent effect on popular Christian spirituality. The narrative tells of how Christian and his friends travel through the 'wilderness of this world' in search of the heavenly city. Bunyan weaves together the imagery of the entry into the Promised Land with that of the new Jerusalem. A river separates us from the heavenly city, just as the River Jordan was placed between Israel and its Promised Land. It is only by crossing this river that access to the city can be gained. In the closing pages of his narrative, Bunyan tells of how Mr Stand-fast prepared to cross the river from this life to the next, trusting that the trumpets would sound for him on the other side: 'I see myself now at the end of my journey, my toilsome days are ended. I am going now to see that head that was crowned with thorns, and that face that was spit upon for me.'[8]

Both Augustine and Bunyan offer their readers a map to help them make sense of the complex and often discouraging experiences of the life of faith. Others have developed similar ideas. A good example can be found in a conference address given by the leading British evangelical preacher and theologian John R. W. Stott (1921–2011). In this lecture, Stott stressed the importance of sustaining the 'hope of heaven' as a means of encouraging Christians to keep going on the long journey of faith. He argued for the recovery of this leading theme of the Christian faith and its application to every aspect of Christian life and thought.

> Lift up your eyes! You are certainly a creature of time, but you are also a child of eternity. You are a citizen of heaven, and an alien and exile on earth, a pilgrim travelling to the celestial city . . . We have important duties on earth, but we must never allow them to preoccupy us in such a way that we forget who we are or where we are going.[9]

Stott invites us to see the journey of faith in terms of *exploring* our faith, appreciating its intellectual richness and its capacity to hold us, encourage us and help us cope with the challenges and discouragement that we will inevitably face along the way. Christian discipleship is shaped on the road of life as we grow into our faith and test it against the challenges and opportunities that come our way. That's why it is so important that we journey in hope!

Worship: sustaining the hope of heaven

One of the ways Christians keep their hope of heaven alive is through worship. Worship is about heightening our awareness of the transcendent aspects of life. It is about seeing through and beyond this everyday world to what lies beyond.

> So if you have been raised with Christ, seek the things that are above, where Christ is, seated at the right hand of God. Set your minds on things that are above, not on things that are on earth, for you have died, and your life is hidden with Christ in God. When Christ who is your life is revealed, then you also will be revealed with him in glory.
>
> (Colossians 3.1–4)

We have already seen how the sacraments help with this process of looking forward with a sense of expectation. Both baptism and the Eucharist recall the past and anticipate the future, which help us live in the present. It's about recalling the family history of the community of faith and looking forward to its final consummation. It's about seeing our own stories in the light of a much greater story and realizing the new dimensions to life that this makes possible.

The Orthodox tradition has long seen the public worship of the Church as drawing close to the threshold of heaven itself and peering through its portals to catch a glimpse of the worship of heaven. The Orthodox liturgy tries to capture the awesome sense of mystery that is evoked by this sense of peering beyond the bounds of human vision. While we are on earth our worship allows us to catch a glimpse of the worship of heaven, which one day we will share.

For Orthodoxy, there is a close link between the Eucharist and the experience of the worship of heaven. The idea of 'liminality' – that is, being on the threshold of the sacred, peering into the distant heavenly realms – is represented visually in the structure of Orthodox churches. For example, the sanctuary and the altar are set apart from the people as a way of expressing the awesomeness of the mystery of God. In their treatises on worship, John Chrysostom (*c.*349–407) and other Greek patristic writers repeatedly draw attention to the liturgical importance of this sense of the sacred. The altar is the 'terrifying table'; the bread and the wine are 'the terrifying sacrifice of the body and blood of Christ which worshippers must approach with fear and trembling'.[10]

These insights, of course, are not limited to Orthodoxy and can be found in some form in most Christian understandings of worship. They are expressed well, for example, in many of the hymns of Charles Wesley. His 'Leader of Faithful Souls' is not sung often these days, but it expresses a traditional understanding of the Christian life in a remarkably accessible manner:

> Strangers and pilgrims here below,
> This earth we know is not our place:
> And hasten through the vale of woe,
> And restless to behold thy face;
> Swift to our heavenly country move,
> Our everlasting home above.[11]

Wesley often uses his hymns to sketch an outline map of the journey of faith through this world to the next. We are 'strangers and pilgrims' on earth. This is not where we really belong, but is a 'vale of woe' through which we must pass, knowing and trusting that we will return home to 'our heavenly country'. This is where we really belong and where we will finally see God, face to face.

Yet we only catch a glimpse of the face of God through worship. Seeing God face to face is one of the privileges of heaven. The Psalmist expressed his longing to see God in words that emphasize the importance of *seeing* God and beholding the divine beauty:

> One thing I asked of the LORD,
>   that will I seek after:
> to live in the house of the LORD
>   all the days of my life,
> to behold the beauty of the LORD.
>   (Psalm 27.4)

The Christian hope is often expressed in terms of seeing the face of God *directly*. In the Old Testament, divine favour is indicated by the face of God being turned towards an individual, just as disfavour is signalled by that face being averted. In cultic petitions of this period, worshippers might invoke God not to turn God's face away as a means of securing the acceptance of the sacrifices or prayers being offered (Psalm 27.9; 132.10). If the face of God were 'hidden' or 'turned away', the believer could have no hope of finding divine acceptance (Deuteronomy 31.17; Ezekiel 7.22).

Yet the image of the 'face of God' concerns far more than the notion of the divine pleasure and favour; it reassures us of the possibility of a personal encounter with the living God. To 'see the face of God' is to have a privileged, intimate relationship with God – seeing God as God actually is (1 John 3.2), rather than having to know God indirectly, through images and shadows. Now we see God as 'through a glass, darkly'; but we shall finally see God 'face to face' (1 Corinthians 13.12 av). The book of Revelation affirms that this will be the privilege of those in heaven, where the saints will finally see God's face (Revelation 22.4).

What about the ascension?

Some readers may feel a little irritation by this stage. Why, they might ask, have I not talked about the ascension? After all, both the Apostles' Creed and the Nicene Creed declare that Jesus of Nazareth 'ascended into heaven and is seated at the right hand of the Father'. It's all very well for us to focus on the Resurrection, but surely something important has been left out here?[12] The Gospels tell us about the death and resurrection of Jesus of Nazareth; our knowledge of the ascension and Pentecost, however, derive primarily from the Acts of the Apostles, widely accepted as having been written by Luke.[13] Here's the account of the ascension as we find it in Acts:

> When [Jesus] had said this, as they were watching, he was lifted up, and a cloud took him out of their sight. While he was going and they were gazing up towards heaven, suddenly two men in white robes stood by them. They said, 'Men of Galilee, why do you stand looking up towards heaven? This Jesus, who has been taken up from you into heaven, will come in the same way as you saw him go into heaven.'
>
> (Acts 1.9–11)

So what's this about, then? The ascension marks the end of the earthly ministry of Jesus of Nazareth. According to Acts, the ascension took place 40 days after the resurrection. For this reason, most churches mark the Feast of the Ascension on a Thursday, not a Sunday – since 40 days after Easter Day, which is always a Sunday, falls on a Thursday. Pentecost follows ten days later. The period between the resurrection and ascension is characterized by meetings between the risen Christ and the disciples. Ascension marks the end of such appearances.

The ascension reinforces one of the most important insights about the identity of Jesus of Nazareth. The death of Jesus of Nazareth on the cross was neither a failure, nor did it mark him out as condemned by God. As the resurrection made clear, Jesus was exalted by God (Ephesians 1.20–23) and given a name that was above all other names (Philippians 2.9). In one sense the ascension is about confirming the identity and significance of Jesus, reinforcing the insights safeguarded by the resurrection. Jesus now stands at the 'right hand' of God – a position of exaltation and influence.[14]

But there's another question we can ask: what difference does it make to us? And here we can begin to map out some very interesting ideas. The most important of these is found in Paul's letters. Jesus of Nazareth, who died, was raised and now stands at the right hand of God, 'intercedes for us' (Romans 8.34). We find this idea elsewhere in the New Testament – for example, the letter to the Hebrews understands intercession as an integral aspect of Jesus of Nazareth's role as high priest: 'Consequently he is able for all time to save those who approach God through him, since he always lives to make intercession for them' (Hebrews 7.25).

As we saw in *Lord and Saviour*, the New Testament understands Jesus of Nazareth to mediate between God and humanity. We naturally tend to think of this primarily in terms of Jesus mediating God to us – for example, in showing us what God is like. Jesus is the 'image of the invisible God' (Colossians 1.15). Or we think in terms of Jesus mediating salvation through his death and resurrection. Yet while we must never lose sight of the importance of these themes, we must never overlook another – namely that the risen Christ represents us to God. He intercedes for us, pleading our case. The first letter of John urges Christians not to sin, yet if things go wrong, there is a way out: 'But if anyone does sin, we have an advocate with the Father, Jesus Christ the righteous' (1 John 2.1).

Yet the creeds set out two additional statements about the Christian hope that we need to consider. One of them concerns the idea of Jesus of Nazareth as king – the one who rules over all things. The Nicene Creed declares that 'his kingdom will have no end'. So what are we to make of that?

The kingly rule of the risen Christ

The theme of the 'kingdom of God' is prominent in the first three Gospels. We all know about the 'parables of the kingdom' – the stories that Jesus of Nazareth told to help his disciples grasp the values and influence of this coming new order. Admittedly the word 'kingdom' needs some nuancing. Most modern readers of the Gospels tend to associate a kingdom with a geographically defined area of land, the area or space ruled by a king. Yet there are very good reasons for thinking that Jesus wanted us to think about the *kingly rule* of God rather than a specific segment of land or territory. The coming of God's reign lies to hand.

Of course, there are some difficulties of interpretation that we need to acknowledge. For example, take the famous words with which Jesus inaugurated his ministry in Galilee: 'The time is fulfilled, and the kingdom of God has come near; repent, and believe in the good news' (Mark 1.15). The most natural reading of this is that since the kingly rule of God is about to dawn, people need to prepare for its coming through repentance. But what sort of kingly rule is this? Was this a reference to a hope of the restoration of the monarchy of Israel, so that a new king would rule over a restored nation?

There is no doubt that at the time of Jesus of Nazareth, when messianic expectations seem to have been at a height, some did believe that. Israel was occupied by Roman forces and had become a province within the Roman Empire. It no longer enjoyed its own distinct national identity, even though Rome tolerated its religious beliefs and practices. Many believed that the Lord God of Israel had promised to establish his sovereign rule over Israel and the world, and that Jesus of Nazareth was somehow involved in embodying this intention.[15] But how? What form would this rule take?

Some seem to have expected Jesus of Nazareth to have become a focus of resistance to Roman occupation. The 'kingdom of God' was thus opposed to the 'kingdom of Caesar'.[16] Throughout the history of Israel, the people of God were oppressed by pagan nations – such as Egypt, the Canaanites, Assyria and Babylon. God's deliverance of Israel from these oppressors was seen by some as establishing a pattern of resistance and eventual triumph. Would Jesus of Nazareth fit this mould? Was he fundamentally a religious and political liberator?

The New Testament answer to this is at once simple and complex. No, Jesus of Nazareth was not a political liberator. What he came to do was to renew and transform the people of God. The Gospels can thus be read in terms of the creation of God's community of renewed individuals, centred around the figure of Jesus and living out this new life together. The 'kingly rule of God' is exercised in both individuals and the community of faith, in whom the risen Christ may be said to 'dwell'. This is not about the creation of a new political realm but about the creation of new people who seek to shape their lives and communities according to the will of God as this is made known in Jesus. To some this seems irritatingly imprecise. Yet the New Testament does not offer a precise account of the nature of the Church, its relationship with the world of politics or an account of the best form of national government.[17]

However, the central themes of the idea of the 'kingly rule of God' can be picked up and developed, by both individuals and churches. We are citizens of another kingdom, and acknowledge its authority over our lives. For the first Christians this meant refusing to acknowledge any other source of supreme authority. If it was a choice between worshipping the Roman emperor and worshipping God, the first Christians chose the latter – and were often martyred for their faithfulness.

Even today Christians are called upon to challenge the ideas and values of our time when we have reason to believe they contradict those of the 'kingdom of God'. The German churches found themselves in this dilemma when Adolf Hitler seized power in Germany in 1933 and began to Nazify German culture. Many Christians were appalled at these developments, especially the blatant discrimination against Jews that followed in their wake. The 'Barmen Declaration' of 1934 issued a challenge to Christians to refuse to conform to such values. Christians were called upon to follow Jesus in an act of intellectual and moral discipleship:

> Jesus Christ, as he is attested for us in Holy Scripture, is the one Word of God which we have to hear and which we have to trust and obey in life and in death. We reject the false teaching, that the Church could and should acknowledge any other events and powers, figures and truths, as God's revelation, or as a source of its proclamation, apart from or in addition to this one Word of God.[18]

Yet there is one more aspect of the Christian hope that we must consider: the return of Jesus of Nazareth as our judge.

So what do the creeds mean when they declare that Jesus 'will come to judge the living and the dead'?

Jesus of Nazareth as judge

Clement of Rome once remarked that Christians must 'think about Jesus Christ as about God, as the judge of the living and the dead'.[19] Traditionally Christians have drawn a distinction between the 'first coming' of Jesus of Nazareth in humility and his 'second coming' in glory as our judge. The Book of Common Prayer (1662) collect for the First Sunday in Advent is rightly admired for its eloquent presentation of these themes:

> Almighty God, give us grace that we may cast away the works of darkness, and put upon us the armour of light, now in the time of this mortal life, in which thy Son Jesus Christ came to visit us in great humility; that in the last day, when he shall come again in his glorious majesty to judge both the quick and the dead, we may rise to the life immortal, through him who liveth and reigneth with thee and the Holy Ghost, now and ever. Amen.[20]

As this collect makes clear, a central theme of the Christian narrative is that the one who will judge us is the one who became incarnate for us. This is no unknown judge but someone who knows us and loves us. We trust Jesus as we trust nobody else to know our deepest secrets and desires, and to do what is best for us.

So what does this mean? Many of us find the word 'judge' alarming as it speaks of our accountability and responsibility. It does not sit easily with the dominant spirit of our age, which is to deny that we're responsible for anything – someone else is always to blame for what's gone wrong with the world, or with my life! As the Polish poet Czesław Miłosz put it, people used to say that religion was opium for the people. But that's changed: 'A true opium for the people is a belief in nothingness after death – the huge solace of thinking that for our betrayals, greed, cowardice, murders we are not going to be judged.'[21] The creeds ask us to take due responsibility for things and not to lay the blame on others. It's unsettling, but it's also honest.

So how does this affect the life of faith? Does this mean that we should be judgemental? After all, if we are to be judged, should we not judge each other? It's not that simple. To judge someone is all too often to see them as inferior to you. A judge is someone who stands above those being judged, who does not share their guilt, failings or vulnerability. The Sermon on the Mount has much that is wise to say to us.

> Do not judge, so that you may not be judged. For with the judgment you make you will be judged, and the measure you give will be the measure you get. Why do you see the speck in your neighbour's eye, but do not notice the log in your own eye? Or how can you say to your neighbour, 'Let me take the speck out of your eye', while the log is in your own eye? You hypocrite, first take the log out of your own eye, and then you will see clearly to take the speck out of your neighbour's eye. (Matthew 7.1–5)

These words of Jesus remind me how easy it is to see myself as superior to others. Yet if I am to judge anyone I must first judge myself and sort myself out. Furthermore I need to see criticism as something *positive* that I can offer – a way of taking something that is good and making it still better. The object of criticism is not to humiliate or demean someone but to enable them to grow and become stronger. It is an act of love, not of power or hostility. My role is to help others to become stronger, not to strengthen my own sense of power or value.

There's one more theme we need to consider in thinking about living out the Christian hope in this life. It's sometimes known as the 'beatific vision' – the idea that we will one day behold God.

Heaven as focusing on God

I get distracted very quickly. I might start reading a book and lose interest after ten pages. Or I might start watching a TV series only to find that it doesn't hold my attention. I often wonder what would happen if I were to encounter something that was so compelling, so wonderful that I would be unable to take my eyes off it.

That's what the Christian hope of finally seeing God face to face is all about. While we are in exile on earth we are not 'fitted' or 'adapted' to beholding the full glory of God; it is only when we ourselves are raised to glory and transformed that we may hope to see the radiance and glory of God in all their fullness. 'We see God according to the measure by which we are adapted to him,' as Augustine of Hippo once remarked. Only when we have been utterly transformed can we hope to see God fully – but, Augustine insisted, it would be worth waiting for! Cyprian of Carthage, martyred for his faith in 258, asked his readers to imagine seeing God in this way, and to take hope from it:

> How great your glory and happiness will be, to be allowed to see God, to be honoured with sharing the joy of salvation and eternal light with Christ your Lord and God, to delight in the joy of immortality in the kingdom of heaven with the righteous and the friends of God.[22]

Our knowledge of God in this life is only a foretaste of the more splendid vision of God that awaits us. We don't see God fully – but we see enough to keep us going and growing in our faith. As C. S. Lewis rightly noted, the Christian hope is about far more than just seeing God; it is about knowing God fully. We may know something of the beauty of God in this world; the best, however, is yet to come:

> We do not want to *see* beauty, though, God knows, that is bounty enough. We want something else which can hardly be put into words – to be united with the beauty we see, to pass into it, to receive it into ourselves, to bathe in it, to become part of it.[23]

In the final chapter we'll look at how you can go about taking things further, opening up ways of enriching your understanding of the faith and making connections with other aspects of the Christian life.

5

Conclusion: further up and further in

———◆•◆•◆———

This series of five books has reflected on the leading themes of the Christian creeds and how these help shape the life of faith. We've looked at the place of doctrine and creeds in the Christian life, as well as exploring some of the basic themes of what Christians believe. We now need to tie together some loose ends as we bring this work to a close.

Faith and the Creeds – the first volume in this series – explained why the creeds were important in helping us grasp the breadth and depth of the Christian faith. They provide a 'rule of faith', a map of the Christian intellectual landscape that both helps us to make sense of our faith and sets our agenda for further exploration of its themes.

We then began to explore the 'rule of faith' in more detail in *The Living God*, which explored the rich Christian understanding of God, focusing especially on the doctrine of the Trinity. While some find this doctrine 'irrational', it really shows up the severe limits of human reason in thinking about the glory and wonder of God. The Christian vision of God goes beyond what human reason can cope with. That's not about being irrational; it's just about realizing how easy it is to become trapped within a rationalist straitjacket. As the great philosopher and intellectual historian Isaiah Berlin once remarked, reason comes to act as a 'prison' that prevents us taking seriously certain important and meaningful thoughts that lie beyond its limited scope. Reason is a good critical tool when used properly – but inadequate as a foundation for the deepest reflections on life.

We then turned to look at the identity and significance of Jesus of Nazareth. In *Lord and Saviour* we considered the central place of Jesus in the Christian faith, including reflecting on the significance of his death on the cross and his resurrection. This led into *The Spirit of Grace*, in which we thought about the role of the Holy Spirit and the place of the Church in the Christian life. And finally, in this volume, we have reflected more fully about the nature of the Christian hope.

This series has tried to have the best of both worlds. On the one hand it has emphasized the importance of seeing the 'big picture' of faith; on the other it has also affirmed and explored its individual components, as these are set out in the creeds of the Christian faith. In this concluding chapter we will reflect on how we might, in C. S. Lewis's words, go 'further up and further in' to the world of the creeds. How can we go deeper into our faith?

To begin with, let's think more about the importance of this idea of a big picture. Why does it matter so much? How does this help us get a deeper grasp of the Christian faith?

Faith: a big picture of reality

A friend of mine likes to be described as a 'detail person'. He's brilliant at gathering vast arrays of facts and organizing them into charts and tables – I doubt if anyone else knows the regulations of the University of Oxford as well as he does. We all need people like this, with masses of information at their fingertips. Working at Oxford University gives me the privilege of having access to people who know far more than I do about the life and thought of important Christian writers like Augustine of Hippo, Thomas Aquinas, Martin Luther and Dorothy L. Sayers – and I value that detail.

Yet the Christian faith is not about being bombarded with details that we have to absorb; it's about grasping the big picture that holds everything together, and subsequently exploring it. The big picture comes first; the details come later. That's how G. K. Chesterton came back to faith after his wilderness experience as an agnostic. His faith didn't depend on this or that specific argument but on the overall intellectual capaciousness of Christianity. Faith is like a garment that could fit snugly on to reality – or at least more snugly than any of its rivals.

It's a point I was helped to grasp some years ago when I stumbled across a sonnet by the American poet Edna St. Vincent Millay (1892–1950). It seemed to her that we were bombarded by 'a meteoric shower of facts' raining from the sky, which lay 'uncombined' on the ground.[1] They were like threads that needed to be woven 'into fabric', dots that needed to be joined together to disclose a picture. Yes we need the detail – and that's why this series has looked at so many individual Christian doctrines. But we also need to apprehend the big picture, which positions these doctrines and helps us see that they are part of a coherent whole rather than disjointed and disconnected individual ideas.

Christian doctrine gives us this big picture, a way of seeing things that helps us make sense of what we observe around us and experience within us. I was drawn to Christianity partly because I sensed it allowed me to grasp and hold on to the intelligibility of our world, an insight expressed in C. S. Lewis's signature affirmation: 'I believe in Christianity as I believe that the Sun has risen, not only because I see it, but because by it, I see everything else.'[2] Yet there is another theme that's important here: the quest for coherence.

Christianity provides a web of meaning, a deep belief in the fundamental interconnectedness of things. It's like standing on top of a mountain and looking down at a patchwork of villages, fields, streams and forests. We can take snapshots of everything we see, yet what we really need is a panorama that holds the snapshots together – that lets us see that there is a big picture and that each of these little pictures has its place within it. The fear of many is that reality consists simply of isolated and disconnected episodes, incidents and observations.

Our modern age has seen doubts about the coherence of reality, many arising from the 'new philosophy' of the Scientific Revolution. Do new scientific ideas destroy any idea of a meaningful reality? The English poet John Donne (1572–1631) spoke movingly of this concern in the early seventeenth century, as scientific discoveries seemed to some to erode any sense of connectedness and continuity within the world: ''Tis all in pieces, all coherence gone,' he wrote of this unsettling new world.[3] How could it be held together?

Christians find this theme eloquently engaged in the New Testament, which speaks of all things holding together or being 'knitted together' in Christ (Colossians 1.17; Ephesians 4.16). There is a hidden web of meaning and connectedness behind the ephemeral and incoherent world that we experience. Christianity provides us with a reassurance of the *coherence of reality* – that however fragmented our world of experience may seem, there is a half-glimpsed 'bigger picture' that holds things together, its threads connecting together in a web of meaning what might otherwise seem incoherent and pointless. This theme resonates throughout the poetic and religious writings of the Middle Ages. As might be expected, it is a major issue in perhaps that greatest of medieval literary classics, Dante's *Divine Comedy*. As the poem draws to its close, Dante catches a glimpse of the unity of the cosmos, in which its aspects and levels are seen to converge into a single whole.[4]

Sir Peter Medawar, a British biologist, thought long and hard about the strengths and limits of science. One of his conclusions stands out for me: 'Only humans find their way by a light that illuminates more than the patch of ground they stand on.'[5] Human beings seem to possess some desire to reach beyond the mechanics of engagement with our world, looking for deeper patterns of significance and meaning. Because we are human beings, we need to set our horizons beyond mere existence, and find *meaning* in what we do.

This does not mean, of course, that such patterns or meaning exist for that reason! Yet there seems to be something about human identity that involves a quest for something deeper. We have seen in this series how Christianity gives us a distinctive way of understanding human nature that helps us grasp both why we long for something deeper and how we come to find it in God. As the novelist Salman Rushdie once rather nicely put it, 'the idea of God' is both 'a repository for our awestruck wonderment at life and an answer to the great questions of existence'.[6]

Yes, doctrines matter, but we need to make sure we never think of Christianity as simply assent to a set of ideas. There is something deeper. Some, such as C. S. Lewis, would find this in the Christian 'metanarrative' – the story of God, which in turn gives rise to doctrines about God. Yet for Lewis, doctrines are always secondary to the story. Others would locate this deeper reality in a relationship or encounter with God, perhaps through reading the Bible. Doctrine is necessary and important but it's not what is *really* important. We believe in God; we believe doctrines. Doctrines help us to avoid the error the poet T. S. Eliot warned against, namely having an experience but missing its proper meaning. We need a framework of interpretation that helps us understand what a story or experience really means.

Christianity offers a big picture of reality, and it is this vision as a whole – rather than any of its individual details – that proves so persuasive and compelling. Lewis was drawn to Christianity for much the same reason as he loved some of the classics of medieval literature: its ability to 'embrace the greatest diversity of subordinated detail'.[7] The Christian faith is best seen as a web of belief in which everything is interconnected and interlocked, rather than as a collection of isolated compartments.

Yet some readers may still have questions about the place of doctrine in the Christian life. Do we really need to worry about these doctrines? Surely all that matters is that we trust and love God! So why do we need doctrine? What difference does it make?

How important are doctrines?

Doctrine aims to make us into faithful disciples. It's not some kind of intellectual optional extra that sets theologians apart from ordinary Christians, but a way of seeing our faith that helps us understand our faith and grow in wisdom. It's about developing habits of thought and action that faithfully reflect and communicate the Christian gospel.

But some people dislike the idea of doctrine. They think that an 'undogmatic Christianity' is, in the first place, possible, and in the second, desirable. Why, some ask, are creeds necessary? After all, they argue, Jesus did not hand on a creed; he taught us simply to love God and our neighbour.

One of the reasons why some people like the idea of an 'undogmatic' Christianity is that the term 'dogmatic' is often understood to mean 'authoritarian'. This is really a complaint about the tone of voice in which Christian theological affirmations are made rather than about their substance – I doubt many people are attracted to shrill, strident, imperious and overbearing assertions of Christian doctrine. But it doesn't have to be like this. Doctrine commends itself; it does not need to assert itself.

Yet in the end it seems to me that a demand for a doctrine-free Christianity is ultimately as unrealistic as it is pointless. Why? Well for a start it amounts to little more than a crude embargo on critical reflection in matters of belief. It asks us not to think about our faith! It represents a retreat from precisely the kind of intellectual engagement that makes Christian theology (and the life of faith) such a genuinely exciting and challenging discipline. Instead of encouraging Christians to think about their faith, it asks us to suspend use of our intellectual faculties in any matters to do with God, Christ or human destiny. Precisely because human beings think, they will want to develop theories about the nature of God and Jesus of Nazareth – and that's a good thing. We want to give the best possible account of our faith! We are, after all, called to love God with all our heart, all our soul and all our mind (Matthew 22.37). Christian theology and doctrines are part of this discipleship of the mind, which supplements – and is not displaced by! – a discipleship of the heart and of the hands.

Doctrines matter. They may not lie at the heart of the Christian faith but they provide us with a framework for thinking about our faith and for explaining its core themes to those outside the churches: 'Coming to see that there is a God involves seeing a new meaning in one's life, and being given a new understanding.'[8] And we can't talk about this 'new meaning' in life or this 'new understanding' of reality without developing and affirming certain beliefs.

Let's be clear that these aren't ideas we've invented. This is not a make-believe world we have created but a faithful and prayerful attempt to express in words something too wonderful and rich to be reduced to words. Christian doctrines try to use words to express and communicate the heartbeat of the Christian faith, knowing they will never fully do justice to their subject but also knowing this has to be done. Down the ages Christians have wrestled with how best to make sense of the Bible and how best to express its ideas in words. And they have passed down to us everything they found helpful and reliable. Rowan Williams expresses this point rather well.

> Doctrinal formulae are neither a set of neat definitions nor some sort of affront to the free-thinking soul; they are words that tell us enough truth to bring us to the edge of speech, and words that sustain enough common life to hold us there together in worship and mutual love.[9]

So how can we grow in our faith? Growth in faith can take the form of a deeper appreciation of our faith – for example, in realizing why the doctrine of the Trinity makes so much sense (for a start, it's about making sure we don't reduce God to what we find intellectually manageable). Yet it can also take the form of discovering new ways of using doctrine.

Who might help us do this? Let's begin by thinking about the role of mentors in the Christian life.

Mentors: people who can help us

We all need older and wiser 'soul friends' to help us think things through. They're further along the road of faith than we are and are often willing to share the wisdom they've gathered. Let me tell you about someone who helped me grow in my faith. As I've mentioned already, I was an atheist who converted to Christianity, studying the natural sciences at Oxford at the time. So how on earth was I to bring together science and my new faith? I needed some help.

I found this when Charles A. Coulson (1910–74), Oxford's first Professor of Theoretical Chemistry – not to be confused with the American politician Charles Colson I mentioned earlier! – preached in my college chapel. Coulson was a fellow of Wadham College, where I was an undergraduate. He was also a prominent Methodist lay preacher who spoke on the fundamental coherence of science and faith. I talked to him afterwards about some of my questions. Coulson helped me see that my new faith did not call upon me to abandon my love of science but to see it in a new way – indeed, to have a new motivation for loving science and a deepened appreciation for its outcomes.[10]

Coulson was my mentor, and I learned a huge amount from talking to him and reading his works. In this series I have drawn on some other writers to help us think about some of the ideas of faith, especially G. K. Chesterton, C. S. Lewis and Dorothy L. Sayers. But there are many others who can help us develop in the life of faith, and you need to find someone who can help you develop in yours. These mentors can help us in a number of ways.

First, each of them has a personal story of discovery to tell. Chesterton, Lewis and Sayers all came to discover the richness of faith, but in different ways. You may find that you can relate to one of them especially well, so that they raise – and answer – questions that matter to you. Chesterton's account of his realization of the way Christianity made sense of his life will speak powerfully to some readers, less so to others. You need to find writers who seem to be on your wavelength, who seem to be attuned to the same questions and concerns as you.

When we reflected on the nature of the Church in *The Spirit of Grace*, I pointed out that Christianity is a corporate faith. We're not meant to fly solo, so to speak, but to grow in faith in company. And that's why reading Christian books is so important. They give us access to wisdom from others who have walked the road of faith before us, and set before us their wisdom and insights so that we can benefit from them. Sometimes we can learn from writers who are still alive; sometimes from those who have completed their journey of faith and now wait for us on another shore. That's why Lewis regarded the reading of Christian classics as so important: it keeps 'the clean sea breeze of the centuries blowing through our minds'.[11]

So who can we learn from? Well that's the hard question, because you need to find out from experience who you find helpful – something only you can answer. You could begin by asking your friends who they read and why they find these writers useful. You could borrow their books and see if you like them. And if you do, try reading more by the same author. Or you could use the web to gain access to texts by classic writers such as Athanasius of Alexandria, Augustine of Hippo, Anselm of Canterbury, Thomas Aquinas, Jonathan Edwards and countless others. There's a world of wisdom waiting to be discovered.

Most of us end up having certain 'soul friends' we keep coming back to. I've already mentioned Charles Coulson; I also owe a great debt to C. S. Lewis. I started reading him in 1974, a few years after I discovered Christianity. I had questions that weren't being answered in the sermons I heard, and I began to ask colleagues who they would recommend me to read if I was to gain a deeper understanding of Christianity. That's how I discovered Lewis, and I have been reading him ever since.

Yet the core themes of the Christian faith impact on our lives in other ways than making sense of our world and helping us to come to terms with its enigmas and ambiguities. One of the most important roles of Christian beliefs is that they give us a moral framework for reflection and action. Let's explore this further.

Ethics: believing and behaving

Christianity is about living, not just thinking. Of course, the way we think affects the way we live, but it's hard to deny that the Gospels and letters of the New Testament are often much more concerned with how Christians behave than with what they should think. Paul's letters, for example, sometimes provide detailed theological reflection as a foundation for the virtues and qualities of the Christian life. His wonderful 'Christ hymn' (Philippians 2), which speaks of

Jesus of Nazareth humbling himself in order to enter our world and redeem us, reinforces his plea for humility on the part of Christians. The way we behave reflects what we believe; ethics rests on theology – but too often we treat these as two separate things that don't interact with each other.

The early Christians often spoke of their faith as a 'philosophy', and regularly depicted Jesus of Nazareth as wearing the traditional garb of a philosopher. Why is this? Surely this amounts to reducing Christianity to a set of ideas? But it's not that straightforward. As the scholar Pierre Hadot has argued, the word 'philosophy' was used in the classical world to mean much more than just abstract thinking. In the classical age, philosophy was seen as *an intellectual expression of a way of life* and as a way of developing a code of conduct reflecting its core values.[12]

When early Christian writers spoke of their faith as a 'philosophy', they understood this not just as a set of ideas but as a way of life leading to wisdom. The supreme example of such a life was, of course, that of Jesus of Nazareth – both his teaching and his lifestyle were seen as the basis of an authentically Christian life. Christians understand Jesus to be both the grounds of our redemption and the model of the redeemed life.

So how does Christian doctrine come into this? The answer is: by helping us see why it is Jesus of Nazareth – and not someone else – who we place at the centre of our moral universe. Dorothy L. Sayers emphasized the importance of this point in her 1940 address, 'Creed or Chaos?' For Sayers, we had to choose who we regarded as our moral authority. Should we obey Jesus of Nazareth or someone else – such as Adolf Hitler?[13] The doctrine of the incarnation tells us what is special about Jesus and why he – and he alone – is our supreme moral example. Theology provides us with a rationale for our moral examples.

But there's a deeper point here, which we need to consider carefully. Christian ethics is not simply a code of moral values; it is a way of behaving that emerges from the big picture of faith. Let's go back to an example I mentioned in *Faith and The Creeds*: the strange stone at Canford School in Dorset.[14] This stone was initially seen as a nuisance, a cumbersome object that served little purpose. It was used in a variety of ways – to prop open doors and as a support for the school's dart board. Then everything suddenly changed when an expert noticed it and realized that this stone was a 3,000-year-old carved panel from the throne room of the Assyrian King Ashurnasirpal II (883–859 BC). As it was now realized to be valuable, it was treated with respect!

Here's the point to note: the way people behaved towards the stone was based on their understanding of its identity. To begin with people saw it as an encumbrance, a useless lump of stone. Then they saw it for what it really was – and their attitude changed. The stone was precious and important. The school took good care of it until it finally sold at auction for nearly $12 million.

The Christian faith gives us a lens through which we see the world, ourselves and other people. We see the world as God's creation – something that belongs to God and matters to God, which has been entrusted to us. And that affects – or ought to affect! – the way we behave towards it. The big picture of the Christian faith allows us to see the world in a new way. A changed understanding of the world leads to a changed attitude towards the world. The creeds give us the basis for a responsible Christian environmental ethic, in that they invite us to see the natural world as something that is special – namely God's beloved creation – so that we realize we must treat it accordingly. They also give us a basis for authentic interpersonal relationships. If we see others as people who bear God's image, for whom Christ died, we will treat them in a new way.

Finally we need to reflect on another way the Christian big picture can be used. In recent years apologetics has become increasingly important to the life and witness of the churches in the West. Movements such as the 'New Atheism' have been severely critical of Christianity – admittedly often on the basis of serious misunderstandings of what the Christian faith is all about. Christians need to know more about their faith and be able to meet challenges to its ideas. Above all they need to be able to explain its core beliefs and express them in ways that people outside the churches can understand. Let's look at these points in more detail.

Apologetics: explaining and commending our faith

Apologetics is the branch of Christian ministry that tries to do three things:

1 show that there are good answers to the problems and concerns people have with the Christian faith;
2 help people outside the Church appreciate the deep appeal of the Christian faith;
3 express the core ideas of the Christian faith in terms that make sense in contemporary culture.

As the recent rise of the New Atheism of Richard Dawkins and others makes clear, it's important to be able to explain what the Christian faith is all about and engage with the questions people ask about it. Perhaps this wouldn't have been all that important two centuries ago when there was a cultural predisposition towards faith in the West; but that's changed and we need to change our attitudes in response. Apologetics is about helping the believer to think and the thinker to believe.

So how does this connect up with the themes of this book? What's the link between the creeds and apologetics? Let's begin by picking up on the idea of a big picture, which we explored especially in *Faith and the Creeds*. Christianity is not like a set of isolated boxes, labelled 'doctrines', but is better seen as a web of interconnecting ideas that help us see that reality is both intelligible and coherent. That's why the idea of the big picture of faith is so important apologetically. The theologian and philosopher Austin Farrer saw clearly why C. S. Lewis's approach to apologetics worked so well: it made its appeal to the imagination, not purely to reason: 'his real power was not proof, it was depiction'. Farrer believed that the success of Lewis's *The Problem of Pain*, published in 1940, lay in its ability to help people see the problem of pain in a new way. Although 'we think we are listening to an argument, in fact we are presented with a vision; and it is the vision that carries conviction'.[15]

Apologetics is grounded in a deep appreciation of the intellectual capaciousness and spiritual richness of the Christian faith. We don't need to make the Christian faith attractive or relevant to the world; rather, we can help people appreciate and discover its relevance and persuasiveness. The best apologetics is always done on the basis of the rich vision of reality that is characteristic of the Christian gospel, which gives rise to deeply realistic insights into human nature. What is our problem? What do we need to do to get things sorted out? In each case a powerful answer may be given to these questions, grounded in the Christian understanding of the nature of things – and expressed in doctrines.

Perhaps a worked example may help us understand how a good understanding of basic Christian theology can help individuals and churches do apologetics more effectively. In *Lord and Saviour* we looked at some basic ideas that were integral to a full appreciation and understanding of the significance of the death of Jesus of Nazareth on the cross.[16] We reflected on five major themes:

- victory over sin and death;
- entering God's presence: the cross as sacrifice;
- ransom;
- the demonstration of divine love;
- forgiveness of sin.

Our concern in *Lord and Saviour* was to understand the theology of these five approaches to the cross. But we're now going to ask a quite different question. What is the apologetic significance of these themes, and how can we use them to help people who don't know very much about Christianity grasp its appeal?

Let me explain what I mean. The question we're asking is how each of these themes could connect up with someone outside the Church. How do they intersect with the deep questions people are asking about the meaning of life or their own personal value? Let's look briefly at each of these five themes and see how we can connect them up with apologetics.

Victory over sin and death One great theme of the gospel is that the cross and resurrection of Jesus of Nazareth free us from the fear of death. This great message of hope in the face of suffering and death has a special relevance to those many people who wake up in the middle of the night, frightened by the thought of death. Many in Western culture are simply unable or unwilling to confront the reality of human mortality. This is the central theme of the cultural anthropologist Ernest Becker's famous book, *The Denial of Death*, published in 1973. Becker argued that many Westerners maintained an illusion of immortality, refusing to concede that they would die one day – it was too difficult and painful a matter to think about and was therefore sidelined and ignored. But it won't go away. For Christians, the cross liberates us from this fear of death and gives us a way of seeing things that sets death in its proper perspective. It is no longer something we need fear.

Entering God's presence: the cross as sacrifice I had to preach once at Westminster Abbey, in the presence of the Queen. I was a little overwhelmed! It's a feeling many will know – a sense that we don't deserve such a privilege. We feel we ought to be very special to enter the presence of someone important. To speak of the 'holiness' of God is to try and express the enormous gap between ourselves as sinners and God as one who is pure and righteous. I know people who have a deep sense of the reality of God but feel unworthy to approach God. You can see how this theme connects up with their concerns: the cross purges us of our guilt so that we are able to enter the presence of God.

Ransom This theme emphasizes that we are trapped in a situation from which we cannot extricate ourselves. Someone else has to set us free – someone who cares enough for us to pay the price this demands. The theme of ransom speaks powerfully to people who know they are trapped and are looking for someone to deliver them. And it invites us to imagine our delight at our freedom, when we are liberated from our place of imprisonment and bondage.

The demonstration of divine love Christians believe in a God who may be trusted, who loves us and who demonstrates that love for humanity in and through the death of Christ on the cross: 'God proves his love for us in that while we still were sinners Christ died for us' (Romans 5.8). We all need a 'secure base' – a context within which we are loved, affirmed and enabled to grow and develop. Families, friends and communities alike have the potential to offer support. Yet many often feel lonely and lost along the road of life, overwhelmed by the thought of the vastness of the universe and the brevity and insignificance of human life. God knows – and loves – each of us by name. That's something many in our culture need to hear, especially when they believe they are worthless and loved by nobody.

Forgiveness of sin Paul declared that 'Christ died for our sins' (1 Corinthians 15.3). It is not just the brute and crude historical fact of the death of Christ that is of such importance; it is what that event means for us. That Jesus died is history; that Jesus died for the forgiveness of our sins is the gospel. For Paul, the cross meant salvation, forgiveness and victory over death. There are many who have such a deep sense of guilt about something they have done – or in some cases have had done to them – that they feel they cannot live properly until the problem has been resolved. How, they wonder, can they achieve this? You can see how those concerns can be connected up with this central theme of the Christian faith – *real forgiveness* of *real sins.*

Now this is just a simple worked example of how a good understanding of Christian beliefs helps us do apologetics, but it's easy to see how this approach could be extended. We could think, for example, about the person of Jesus of Nazareth. What does it mean to say he is our saviour, our friend, our Lord? How might these terms help other people grasp something of what Christianity has to say and how this might connect up with their hopes and fears? There is much that could be said here! Maybe this series of books will help you develop your own approach.

Finally, we need to say a little more about the importance of translating Christian doctrines into everyday English. How can we express the great doctrines of the Christian faith in language that our culture can understand, and connect up with the longings, aspirations and concerns of the world around us? C. S. Lewis expressed the same idea more clearly, when he urged his readers to translate their theology into the ordinary language of their day: 'We must learn the language of our audience.'[17] And that means taking trouble to try and explain key Christian ideas – such as the incarnation or atonement – using analogies, stories and language that a secular audience can understand. 'You must translate every bit of your Theology into the vernacular,' Lewis declared. 'Power to translate is the test of having really understood one's own meaning.'[18]

So what stories might we tell to illustrate the idea of redemption? What analogies might we use to try and help people grasp what the doctrine of the Trinity or the incarnation is all about? In these five volumes, I've used quite a few! Let me invite *you* to think about what you would say if someone asked you to tell them what Christians think is so special about Good Friday or what they mean when they talk about heaven.

Conclusion

It's time to bring this volume – and this Christian Belief for Everyone series – to an end. I have tried to help you grasp and appreciate at least something of the remarkable Christian vision of reality, and see how the Christian creeds give us a framework for understanding who we are and how we can live meaningful lives in this world. There is so much more that needs to be said! I am very aware that I have failed to do justice to the richness of the topics we've been considering. You may well feel some sympathy for the village congregations who so patiently and graciously listened to my sermons!

Yet I hope that what I have presented, though limited in so many ways, may still be encouraging and helpful. Perhaps these five volumes are best seen as a 'taster', an encouragement to go deeper and further into the rich fabric of faith. But I hope that this short series will whet your appetite and encourage you to take your reading and thinking further.

Thank you for your company on this journey of exploration and discovery.

Notes

Introduction

1 John Dewey, *The Quest for Certainty*. New York: Capricorn Books, 1960, 255.

1 The sacraments: signs and memories of hope

1 For a good introduction to the issues, see Alister E. McGrath, *Christian Theology: An Introduction*. Oxford: Wiley-Blackwell, 2011, 400–23; Andrew Davison, *Why Sacraments?* London: SPCK, 2013.

2 For these oaths, see Luca Grillo, *The Art of Caesar's Bellum Civile: Literature, Ideology, and Community*. Cambridge: Cambridge University Press, 2012, 58–76.

3 C. S. Lewis, *Mere Christianity*. London: HarperCollins, 2002, 64.

4 See the excellent study of Hans Urs von Balthasar, *Scandal of the Incarnation: Irenaeus against the Heresies*. San Francisco: Ignatius Press, 1990.

5 John Calvin, *Institutes of the Christian Religion*, IV.xiv.1. For a discussion, see Ronald S. Wallace, *Calvin's Doctrine of the Word and Sacrament*. Edinburgh: Scottish Academic Press, 1995.

6 C. S. Lewis, *Surprised by Joy*. London: HarperCollins, 2002, 221–2.

7 Christian Smith, *Moral, Believing Animals: Human Personhood and Culture*. Oxford: Oxford University Press, 2009, 64.

8 Matthias Reinhard Hoffman, *The Destroyer and the Lamb: The Relationship Between Angelomorphic and Lamb Christology in the Book of Revelation*. Tübingen: Mohr Siebeck, 2005, 113–24.

9 For the significance of the Temple Mount, see Yaron Z. Eliav, *God's Mountain: The Temple Mount in Time, Place, and Memory.* Baltimore: Johns Hopkins University Press, 2005.

10 See the careful study of Jacob Wright, *Rebuilding Identity: The Nehemiah-Memoir and its Earliest Readers.* Berlin: Walter de Gruyter, 2004.

11 Tertullian, *On Baptism*, I, 9. See further Everett Ferguson, *Baptism in the Early Church: History, Theology, and Liturgy in the First Five Centuries.* Grand Rapids, MI: Eerdmans, 2008.

12 Martin Luther, *Shorter Catechism*, 4.

13 See further Jerome Kodell, *The Eucharist in the New Testament.* Collegeville, MN: Liturgical Press, 1991; Eugene LaVerdiere, *The Eucharist in the New Testament and the Early Church.* Collegeville, MN: Liturgical Press, 1996.

14 Council of Trent, *Decree on the Most Holy Sacrament of the Eucharist*, ch. 1.

15 Council of Trent, *Decree*, ch. 4.

16 Thomas Aquinas, *Summa Theologiae*, IIIa q. 75, a. 5.

2 The resurrection of the dead

1 See further N. T. Wright, *The Resurrection of the Son of God.* London: SPCK, 2003.

2 George Herbert, 'Easter', in *Complete English Poems.* London: Penguin, 2004, 35.

3 For a good introduction to this theme in the New Testament, see Richard N. Longenecker, *Life in the Face of Death: The Resurrection Message of the New Testament.* Grand Rapids, MI: Eerdmans, 1998. More generally, see Christopher Morse, *The Difference Heaven Makes: Rehearing the Gospel as News.* London: T&T Clark, 2010; Alister E. McGrath, *Christian Theology: An Introduction.* Oxford: Wiley-Blackwell, 2011, 444–63.

4 James D. G. Dunn, 'A Light to the Gentiles: The Significance of the Damascus Road Theophany for Paul', in *The Glory of Christ in the New Testament*, ed. L. D. Hurst and N. T. Wright. Oxford:

Oxford University Press, 1987, 21–36; Richard N. Longenecker, *The Road from Damascus: The Impact of Paul's Conversion on His Life, Thought, and Ministry*. Grand Rapids, MI: Eerdmans, 1997.

5 Jonathan Aitken, *Charles W. Colson: A Life Redeemed*. New York: Waterbrook Press, 2005.

6 Dorothy L. Sayers, *The Greatest Drama Ever Staged*. London: Hodder & Stoughton, 1938, 5.

7 Frederick Buechner, *The Magnificent Defeat*. San Francisco: HarperOne, 1986, 18.

8 Buechner, *The Magnificent Defeat*, 99.

9 Buechner, *The Magnificent Defeat*, 35.

10 See 'The Cross, Suffering, and Spiritual Bewilderment: Reflections on Martin Luther and C. S. Lewis', in Alister McGrath, *Mere Theology: Christian Faith and the Discipleship of the Mind*. London: SPCK, 2010, 39–49.

11 For a more academic presentation of these ideas, see Alister E. McGrath, *Luther's Theology of the Cross: Martin Luther's Theological Breakthrough*, 2nd edn. Oxford: Wiley-Blackwell, 2011, 201–28.

12 *Bridget Jones: The Edge of Reason* (2004), directed by Beeban Kidron, starring Renée Zellweger, Colin Firth and Hugh Grant. The movie is based on Helen Fielding's 1999 novel with the same title.

13 Methodius of Olympus, *On the Resurrection*, I.xlii.1–xliii.4.

14 <http://billygraham.org/answer/when-a-christian-dies-is-it-all-right-to-cremate-the-body>.

15 <http://billygraham.org/answer/when-a-christian-dies-is-it-all-right-to-cremate-the-body>.

16 Bonaventure, *Breviloquium*, vii, 5.

3 Heaven and eternity: the Christian hope

1 Mary Midgley, *Evolution as a Religion: Strange Hopes and Stranger Fears*, 2nd edn. London: Routledge, 2002, 17–18.

2 C. S. Lewis, *Mere Christianity*. London: HarperCollins, 2002, 134.

3 C. S. Lewis, *Surprised by Joy*. London: HarperCollins, 2002, 221–2.

4 Joseph Addison, *Cato*, Act 1, Scene 5. *The Works of Joseph Addison*, 5 vols. New York: Harper, 1837, vol. 3, 497.

5 G. K. Chesterton, *The Everlasting Man*. San Francisco: Ignatius Press, 1993, 211.

6 See Philip Johnston, *Shades of Sheol: Death and Afterlife in the Old Testament*. Nottingham: Inter-Varsity Press, 2002.

7 Ben Witherington III, *Revelation*. Cambridge: Cambridge University Press, 2003, 1–40.

8 Andrew T. Lincoln. *Paradise Now and Not Yet: Studies in the Role of the Heavenly Dimension in Paul's Thought with Special Reference to His Eschatology*. Cambridge: Cambridge University Press, 2004.

9 Martin Goodman, 'Paradise, Gardens and the Afterlife in the First Century CE', in *Paradise in Antiquity: Jewish and Christian Views*, ed. Markus Bockmuehl and Guy G. Strousma. Cambridge: Cambridge University Press, 2010, 15–39.

10 J. R. R. Tolkien, *The Return of the King*. London: Allen & Unwin, 1966, 199.

11 Jean-Christophe Dufau, 'Mythic Space in Tolkien's Work (*The Lord of the Rings*, *The Hobbit* and *The Silmarillion*)', in *Reconsidering Tolkien*, ed. Thomas Honegger. Zurich: Walking Tree Press, 2005, 107–28.

12 See Alister E. McGrath, *C. S. Lewis: A Life*. London: Hodder & Stoughton, 2013, 22–3.

13 Lewis, *Mere Christianity*, 136–7.

14 Lewis, *Surprised by Joy*, 258.

15 C. S. Lewis, *The Last Battle*. London: HarperCollins, 2004, 171.

16 Letter to Mary Willis Shelburne, 28 June 1963; C. S. Lewis, *Collected Letters*, 3 vols. San Francisco: HarperOne, 2004–6, vol. 3, 1434. Emphasis in original.

17 G. K. Chesterton, *Tremendous Trifles*. London: Methuen, 1909, 209. Emphasis in original.

18 Frederick Buechner, *The Magnificent Defeat*. San Francisco: HarperOne, 1986, 91.

19 Chad Schrock, 'She Came Down from Heaven: The Storied Propositions of Piers Plowman's Holy Church'. *Literature and Theology* 28 (2014): 1–14.

20 For discussion, see John Laansma, '"I Will Give You Rest": The Background and Significance of the Rest Motif in the New Testament'. *Tyndale Bulletin* 46:2 (1995): 385–8.

21 Hillary Kelleher, '"Light Thy Darknes Is": George Herbert and Negative Theology'. *George Herbert Journal* 28:1 and 2 (2005): 47–64.

4 Between the times: the life of faith

1 Matthew Arnold, *Poems*. London: Macmillan, 1878, 338.

2 See Paula Gooder, *Heaven*. London: SPCK, 2011.

3 See, for example, John Pritchard, *The Journey*. London: SPCK, 2014.

4 *The Works of Jonathan Edwards*, 2 vols. London: William Ball, 1839, vol. 2, 244. The emphasis is in the original.

5 C. S. Lewis, *Mere Christianity*. London: HarperCollins, 2002, 137.

6 Robert Dodaro, 'Augustine's Secular City', in *Augustine and His Critics: Essays in Honour of Gerald Bonner*, ed. Robert Dodaro and George Lawless. London: Routledge, 2000, 231–59.

7 For some excellent studies of Bunyan, see Anne Dunan-Page (ed.), *The Cambridge Companion to Bunyan*. Cambridge: Cambridge University Press, 2010.

8 John Bunyan, *The Pilgrim's Progress*. London: Vallance & Simmons, 1878, 175.

9 John Stott, 'The Biblical Basis for Declaring God's Glory', in *Declare His Glory Among the Nations*, ed. David M. Howard. Downers Grove, IL: InterVarsity Press, 1977, 29–91.

10 John Chrysostom, *Homily 24*, 8.

11 Hymn 47, *A Pocket Hymn Book for the Use of Christians of All Denominations*, 11th edn. London, 1794, 49.

12 For a good account, see Paula Gooder, *This Risen Existence: The Spirit of Easter*. Norwich: Canterbury Press, 2011, 94–109.

13 Arie W. Zwiep, *The Ascension of the Messiah in Lukan Christology*. Leiden: Brill, 1997.

14 Andrew Chester, *Messiah and Exaltation: Jewish Messianic and Visionary Traditions and New Testament Christology*. Tübingen: Mohr Siebeck, 2007.

15 See the major recent study by N. T. Wright, *How God Became King: Getting to the Heart of the Gospels*. London: SPCK, 2012.

16 Wright, *How God Became King*, 127–54.

17 R. T. France, *Divine Government: God's Kingship in the Gospel of Mark*. London: SPCK, 1990.

18 Wilhelm Niesel (ed.), *Bekenntnisschriften und Kirchenordnungen der nach Gottes Wort reformierten Kirche*. Zurich: Evangelischer Verlag, 1938, 335–6. The translation is mine.

19 2 Clement 1.1. This letter was probably written in the early second century.

20 'Quick' is an older English word that we would now translate as 'living'.

21 Czesław Miłosz, 'Discreet Charm of Nihilism'. *New York Times*, 19 November 1998.

22 Cyprian, *Letter* 58, 10.

23 C. S. Lewis, 'The Weight of Glory', in *Essay Collection*. London: HarperCollins, 2002, 99.

5 Conclusion: further up and further in

1 Edna St. Vincent Millay, untitled, in *Collected Sonnets*. New York: Harper, 1988, 140.

2 C. S. Lewis, 'Is Theology Poetry?', in *Essay Collection*. London: HarperCollins, 2002, 21.

3 John Donne, 'The First Anniversarie: An Anatomy of the World', line 213, in W. Milgate (ed.), *The Epithalamions, Anniversaries and Epicedes of John Donne*. Oxford: Clarendon Press, 1978, 28.

4 Dante, *Paradiso* XXXIII, 85–90.

5 Peter B. Medawar and Jean Medawar, *The Life Science: Current Ideas of Biology*. London: Wildwood House, 1977, 171.

6 Salman Rushdie, *Is Nothing Sacred? The Herbert Read Memorial Lecture 1990*. Cambridge: Granta, 1990, 8.

7 C. S. Lewis, *The Allegory of Love*. London: Oxford University Press, 1936, 142.

8 D. Z. Phillips, *Faith and Philosophical Enquiry*. London: Routledge & Kegan Paul, 1970, 17.

9 Rowan Williams, *Wrestling With Angels: Conversations in Modern Theology*. London: SCM Press, 2007, xiv.

10 C. A. Coulson, *Science and Christian Belief*. London: Oxford University Press, 1955, 97–102. For my own way of thinking on these questions, see Alister McGrath, *Inventing the Universe: Why We Can't Stop Talking about Science, Faith and God*. London: Hodder & Stoughton, 2015.

11 C. S. Lewis, 'On the Reading of Old Books', in *Essay Collection*, 440.

12 Pierre Hadot, *What Is Ancient Philosophy?* Cambridge, MA: Harvard University Press, 2002, 3–4; *Philosophy as a Way of Life: Spiritual Exercises from Socrates to Foucault*. Malden, MA: Blackwell, 1995, 49–70.

13 Dorothy L. Sayers, 'Creed or Chaos?', in *Creed or Chaos? and Other Essays in Popular Theology*. London: Methuen, 1947, 24.

14 Alister McGrath, *Faith and the Creeds*. London: SPCK, 2013, 26–8.

15 Austin Farrer, 'The Christian Apologist', in *Light on C. S. Lewis*, ed. Jocelyn Gibb. London: Geoffrey Bles, 1965, 23–43. Although Farrer refers specifically to *The Problem of Pain*, the same approach is found throughout Lewis's apologetic writings.

16 Alister McGrath, *Lord and Saviour: Jesus of Nazareth*. London: SPCK, 2014, 75–98.

17 C. S. Lewis, 'Christian Apologetics', in *Essay Collection*, 153.

18 Lewis, 'Christian Apologetics', in *Essay Collection*, 155.